Natural Magick: Buer's Rituals for Health and Harmony

By

Dorian Bloodmoon

Table of Contents

Part III: Rituals for Health and Harmony

Part IV: Mental and Emotional Wellness

Part V: Spiritual Growth and Enlightenment

Conclusion

Dedication

To Buer,

With deep gratitude and reverence, I dedicate this book to you. Your timeless wisdom and healing touch have guided me through the paths of natural magick, illuminating the way with your profound knowledge and gentle spirit. Your teachings have not only enriched my practice but also brought harmony and wellness into my life.

May this book serve as a testament to your boundless compassion and your unwavering commitment to those who seek your guidance. Your presence has been a source of strength and inspiration, and I am honored to share your wisdom with others.

Thank you for your benevolence, your lessons, and your unwavering support. This work is a reflection of your influence, and I hope it will help others find the same healing and enlightenment that you have bestowed upon me.

With deepest respect and devotion,
Dorian Bloodmoon

Legal Disclaimer

The information and practices outlined in this book, "Natural Magick: Buer's Rituals for Health and Harmony," are intended for educational and inspirational purposes only. The results you may achieve through the use of the techniques, rituals, and suggestions presented herein can vary significantly depending on your individual work ethic, commitment, and personal circumstances.

It is important to note that while many people find great benefit and positive outcomes from engaging in natural magick and spiritual practices, these results are not guaranteed. Success in any form of magickal or spiritual work requires consistent effort, dedication, and an open mind. The effectiveness of the rituals and remedies described in this book will depend largely on your personal engagement with the material, your intent, and your adherence to the instructions provided.

Furthermore, the content of this book is not intended as a substitute for professional medical advice, diagnosis, or treatment. Always seek the advice of your physician or other qualified health provider with any questions you may have regarding a medical condition. Never disregard professional medical advice or delay seeking it because of something you have read in this book.

By using the information in this book, you acknowledge and accept that the authors, publishers, and distributors are not responsible for any outcomes or results that may arise from your use of the material. Your success with natural magick and healing practices is ultimately your responsibility and is influenced by your own efforts and circumstances.
May your journey with natural magick be fulfilling and bring you health, harmony, and personal growth.

Chapter 1: Welcome to Natural Magick: Understanding Buer's Wisdom and Healing Traditions

Welcome to a transformative journey into the heart of natural magick, where the ancient wisdom of the Goetic spirit Buer intertwines with the timeless traditions of healing and harmony. In this book, you will discover the profound teachings of Buer, a Great President of Hell, who offers unparalleled knowledge in moral philosophy, natural sciences, and the healing arts. Whether you are a seasoned practitioner or new to the world of magick, Buer's insights will illuminate your path to physical, mental, and spiritual well-being.

Who is Buer?

In the mystical pantheon of the Lesser Key of Solomon, Buer stands out as a figure of great significance and benevolence. Unlike many spirits often depicted with fearsome attributes, Buer is celebrated for his wisdom and his willingness to impart knowledge that enhances the quality of life. Traditionally depicted as a centaur or a lion-headed being with multiple legs, his form symbolizes his multifaceted nature and his ability to navigate various realms of knowledge and healing.

Buer commands fifty legions of spirits, a testament to his power and authority. Yet, it is his role as a teacher and healer that endears him to those who seek his guidance. His teachings encompass moral philosophy, which aids in ethical living; natural philosophy, which offers a deeper understanding of the world; and the healing arts, which promote health and well-being. By connecting with Buer, you open yourself to a wealth of knowledge that has been revered for centuries.

The Essence of Natural Magick

Natural magick, at its core, is about harnessing the inherent energies of the natural world to bring about change, healing, and harmony. Unlike ceremonial magick, which often involves elaborate rituals and complex tools, natural magick is rooted in simplicity and accessibility. It relies on the power of herbs, stones, elements, and the practitioner's intent. Through this form of magick, we seek to align ourselves with the rhythms of nature, drawing on its wisdom and strength to enhance our lives.

In this book, we focus on the specific branch of natural magick guided by Buer's teachings. You will learn how to create healing potions and remedies using herbs, perform rituals that promote health and protection, and cultivate a spiritual practice that fosters balance and peace. By following Buer's guidance, you will not only develop your skills as a magickal practitioner but also enhance your overall well-being.

The Journey Ahead

As we embark on this journey together, it's important to approach the practice with an open mind and a willing heart. The path of natural magick is one of continuous learning and personal growth. Each chapter in this book is designed to build upon the last, gradually deepening your understanding and expanding your capabilities.

We will begin by exploring the historical and philosophical foundations of Buer's teachings. Understanding the roots of these traditions will provide you with a solid grounding and a sense of connection to the ancient wisdom that underpins natural magick. From there, we will delve into practical applications, including the preparation of herbal remedies, the performance of daily rituals, and the creation of protective charms and talismans.

The Power of Herbs and Natural Remedies

One of the cornerstones of Buer's teachings is the use of herbs for healing and protection. Herbs have been used for centuries across cultures for their medicinal properties and their ability to carry magickal intent. In this book, you will learn to identify, gather, and prepare herbs that are potent allies in your practice. Each herb has its own unique properties and associations, and understanding these will enable you to create powerful remedies and spells.

For example, lavender is well-known for its calming properties and can be used in rituals to promote peace and relaxation. Rosemary, on the other hand, is a powerful protector and purifier, ideal for cleansing spaces and warding off negative energies. By working with these natural allies, you will be able to address a wide range of physical and spiritual needs.

Rituals for Health and Harmony

Rituals are a vital aspect of natural magick, providing structure and focus for your intentions. In this book, you will find detailed instructions for a variety of rituals designed to enhance your health and bring harmony into your life. These rituals are accessible and can be performed with simple tools and ingredients.

One such ritual is the Healing Circle, which involves creating a sacred space, invoking Buer's presence, and using herbs and candles to promote physical and emotional healing. Another is the Protection Charm, a small talisman crafted with specific herbs and symbols to safeguard you and your home from harm. These rituals not only bring about tangible results but also deepen your connection to the natural world and the spiritual forces that guide you.

Integrating Spiritual and Physical Practices

True health and harmony come from the integration of the physical and the spiritual. Buer's teachings emphasize the importance of maintaining balance in all aspects of life. This holistic approach is reflected in the practices and rituals outlined in this book. You will learn to listen to your body, mind, and spirit, addressing the needs of each with care and intention.

Meditation and mindfulness are key components of this integration. By cultivating a daily practice of meditation, you will enhance your ability to focus, reduce stress, and open yourself to spiritual insights. Guided meditations included in this book will help you connect with Buer and receive his guidance directly. These practices will support your overall well-being and enhance the effectiveness of your magickal work.

Ethical Considerations and Respect for the Natural World

As we engage in natural magick, it is crucial to approach our practice with respect and ethical consideration. The natural world is a source of incredible power and wisdom, and we must honor it by using our skills responsibly. This means gathering herbs sustainably, treating the spirits and energies we work with respectfully, and using our magick for positive and constructive purposes.

Buer's teachings also include ethical philosophy, providing guidance on how to live in harmony with others and the world around us. By following these principles, you will not only become a more effective practitioner but also contribute to a more balanced and compassionate world.

Continuing Your Journey

This book is a starting point for your exploration of natural magick with Buer. As you progress through the chapters, you will gain a deeper understanding and develop your skills. However, the journey does not end here. The practice of magick is a lifelong path, filled with continuous learning and personal growth.

We encourage you to keep a journal of your experiences, noting the insights and results you achieve. This will not only help you track your progress but also provide valuable reflections that you can revisit in the future. Additionally, seek out communities of like-minded practitioners. Sharing your journey with others can offer support, inspiration, and new perspectives.

Conclusion

In "Natural Magick: Buer's Rituals for Health and Harmony," you are invited to explore a path of profound transformation and healing. By embracing Buer's wisdom and integrating natural magick into your life, you will unlock the potential for true harmony and well-being. This journey is one of discovery, empowerment, and connection to the ancient traditions that continue to offer guidance and insight. We welcome you to this journey and look forward to walking this path with you. May Buer's wisdom light your way, and may you find health, harmony, and magick in every step.

Chapter 2: The History of Healing Magick

The Dawn of Healing Magick

The art of healing magick is as old as humanity itself, born from our ancestors' deep connection with the natural world. Long before the advent of modern medicine, ancient civilizations turned to the earth's bounty for remedies and cures.

The practice of healing magick, rooted in the symbiotic relationship between humans and nature, has evolved over millennia, weaving through various cultures and traditions. In this chapter, we will embark on a journey through time, exploring the rich history of healing magick and its enduring relevance in our lives today.

Ancient Roots: The Beginnings of Healing Magick

Our journey begins in the prehistoric era, where early humans relied on their keen observation of the natural world to survive. They learned to recognize the healing properties of plants, minerals, and other natural elements through trial and error. These early practitioners of healing magick were the shamans, medicine men, and wise women who acted as the healers and spiritual leaders of their communities.

The shamanic traditions of indigenous cultures worldwide are among the earliest recorded practices of healing magick. Shamans used their deep connection with the spirit world to diagnose and treat illnesses, employing a combination of herbal remedies, rituals, and spiritual guidance. They believed that health was a state of balance between the physical, emotional, and spiritual realms, and that illness was a manifestation of disharmony within this delicate equilibrium.

Ancient Egypt: The Intersection of Medicine and Magick

As we move forward in time, we arrive in ancient Egypt, a civilization renowned for its advanced knowledge of medicine and magick. Egyptian healers, known as "swnw," were skilled in the use of herbs, surgery, and magickal incantations. The Ebers Papyrus, one of the oldest medical texts in existence, provides a glimpse into the extensive pharmacopeia and healing practices of ancient Egypt.

Egyptian healers believed that magick was an essential component of medicine. They invoked the gods and goddesses, particularly Isis and Thoth, to aid in their healing work. Amulets, charms, and magickal spells were commonly used to protect patients from malevolent spirits and to enhance the effectiveness of treatments. The integration of magick and medicine in ancient Egypt highlights the holistic approach to healing that remains relevant in modern natural magick practices.

The Greco-Roman Era: Foundations of Western Medicine and Magick

The Greco-Roman era marks a significant period in the history of healing magick, where the foundations of Western medicine were laid. Figures such as Hippocrates and Galen are celebrated for their contributions to medical science, yet their practices were deeply intertwined with magickal beliefs.

Hippocrates, often referred to as the "Father of Medicine," emphasized the importance of natural remedies and the healing power of nature. His holistic approach to medicine recognized the body's innate ability to heal itself, a principle that resonates with the practices of natural magick today. Galen, a prominent physician in the Roman Empire, expanded on Hippocrates' work and incorporated magickal elements into his treatments, such as the use of amulets and astrological influences.

The Greco-Roman era also saw the rise of Hermeticism, a philosophical and spiritual tradition attributed to Hermes Trismegistus. Hermetic texts, such as the Corpus Hermeticum, explored the connections between the microcosm (the human body) and the macrocosm (the universe), emphasizing the importance of harmony between the two. This Hermetic principle is a cornerstone of natural magick, underscoring the belief that healing involves aligning oneself with the greater forces of the cosmos.

Medieval and Renaissance Europe: The Revival of Magickal Healing

The Middle Ages and the Renaissance were periods of both suppression and resurgence for healing magick. During the medieval era, the rise of Christianity led to the persecution of many traditional healers, who were often accused of witchcraft and heresy. However, despite the Church's efforts to eradicate magickal practices, the knowledge of herbal medicine and healing magick persisted, passed down through generations in secret.

The Renaissance, with its renewed interest in classical knowledge, brought about a revival of magickal healing. Alchemists, astrologers, and magicians such as Paracelsus and John Dee sought to bridge the gap between science and magick. Paracelsus, a Swiss physician and alchemist, is particularly noteworthy for his contributions to both medicine and magick. He advocated for the use of chemical compounds and herbal remedies, and his work laid the groundwork for modern pharmacology. Paracelsus believed that true healing required understanding the spiritual causes of illness and addressing them through magickal means.

John Dee, an English mathematician, astrologer, and magus, exemplified the Renaissance synthesis of science and magick. His work with Enochian magick, a system of angelic communication, aimed to uncover the hidden knowledge of the universe. Dee's holistic approach to healing, which integrated magick, astrology, and natural philosophy, reflects the enduring relevance of these practices in contemporary natural magick.

The Enlightenment and Beyond: The Marginalization of Magick

The Enlightenment era, with its emphasis on reason and empirical science, marked a turning point in the history of healing magick. As modern medicine advanced, magickal practices were increasingly marginalized and dismissed as superstition. The rise of industrialization and the scientific method led to a more mechanistic view of the human body, focusing on physical symptoms and treatments while neglecting the spiritual and emotional aspects of healing.

Despite this shift, the 19th and 20th centuries saw a resurgence of interest in magickal healing, particularly within the context of occultism and the New Age movement. Figures such as Aleister Crowley and the members of the Hermetic Order of the Golden Dawn sought to revive and modernize ancient magickal practices. The Golden Dawn, in particular, played a pivotal role in the revival of ceremonial magick and the integration of healing practices within this framework.

Contemporary Natural Magick: A Holistic Approach to Healing

In the modern era, there is a growing recognition of the limitations of purely mechanistic approaches to health and a renewed interest in holistic healing practices. Natural magick, with its emphasis on the interconnectedness of the physical, emotional, and spiritual realms, offers a comprehensive approach to well-being.

Contemporary practitioners of natural magick draw on the rich traditions of the past, integrating ancient wisdom with modern insights. Herbal medicine, energy healing, and magickal rituals are employed to address a wide range of health issues, from chronic illnesses to emotional imbalances. The resurgence of interest in natural magick reflects a broader cultural shift towards sustainability, mindfulness, and a deeper connection with the natural world.

Buer's Role in Healing Magick

Buer, as a Goetic spirit associated with healing, philosophy, and natural sciences, plays a significant role in the practice of natural magick. His teachings encompass a wide range of healing modalities, from the use of herbs and natural remedies to the application of ethical and philosophical principles in everyday life. By invoking Buer's wisdom, practitioners can enhance their understanding of the natural world and harness its healing energies.

Buer's emphasis on moral philosophy also underscores the ethical considerations inherent in magickal healing. Practitioners are encouraged to approach their work with integrity, respect for the natural world, and a commitment to the well-being of others. This holistic approach aligns with the core principles of natural magick, emphasizing balance, harmony, and the interconnectedness of all things.

Conclusion: The Enduring Legacy of Healing Magick

The history of healing magick is a testament to humanity's enduring quest for health, harmony, and a deeper understanding of the natural world. From the shamanic traditions of ancient cultures to the sophisticated practices of contemporary magicians, healing magick has evolved and adapted, remaining relevant across the ages.

In "Natural Magick: Buer's Rituals for Health and Harmony," we will delve deeper into the practical applications of Buer's teachings, exploring how you can incorporate these ancient practices into your modern life. By embracing the wisdom of healing magick, you can unlock the potential for true well-being, aligning yourself with the natural rhythms of the earth and the greater forces of the cosmos.

As we continue this journey together, remember that the path of healing magick is one of continuous learning and growth. May the wisdom of Buer guide you, and may you find health, harmony, and magick in every step.

Chapter 3: Connecting with Buer The Spirit of Wisdom and Healing

In the realm of Goetic spirits, Buer stands as a beacon of wisdom, healing, and enlightenment. Connecting with Buer is not merely about summoning a spirit; it's about establishing a profound relationship that can transform your understanding of natural magick and elevate your spiritual practice. This chapter will guide you through the essential steps to forge a connection with Buer, offering practical rituals, meditative practices, and insights into the spirit's nature and teachings.

Understanding Buer

Buer, one of the 72 spirits of the Ars Goetia, is known for his vast knowledge in philosophy, medicine, and natural sciences. Depicted often as a centaur or a unique being with multiple legs radiating from a central point, his form symbolizes his ability to traverse multiple realms of knowledge and existence. Commanding 50 legions of spirits, Buer is a powerful entity whose guidance can lead to profound personal and spiritual growth.

What sets Buer apart is his benevolence and his desire to impart wisdom. Unlike some spirits whose nature might be more capricious, Buer's teachings focus on healing, both physical and spiritual, and on imparting ethical and philosophical understanding. Engaging with Buer means opening yourself to a mentor who can help you navigate the complexities of life with a balanced and enlightened perspective.

Preparing for Connection

Before attempting to connect with Buer, it is crucial to prepare both your physical space and your mental state. Here are some steps to ensure you are ready:

1. **Create a Sacred Space**: Choose a quiet, undisturbed area where you can perform rituals and meditations. Cleanse this space physically and energetically using sage, incense, or your preferred method of purification.
2. **Gather Necessary Tools**: For rituals involving Buer, you might need items such as candles (preferably in colors associated with healing, like green or blue), herbs, crystals, and a journal to document your experiences.

3. **Mental Preparation**: Entering into a relationship with a spirit requires mental clarity and openness. Spend some time in meditation, focusing on your intention to connect with Buer. Clear your mind of distractions and ground yourself.

The Ritual of Invocation

The invocation ritual is a formal way to invite Buer into your sacred space and establish a connection. Here's a step-by-step guide:

1. **Set the Scene**: Light the candles and incense in your sacred space. Arrange any tools or offerings you have chosen to honor Buer.
2. **Draw the Sigil**: Buer's sigil is a powerful symbol that acts as a gateway for his presence. Draw it on a piece of paper or parchment and place it in front of you.

3. **Invoke Buer**: Begin by reciting an invocation to Buer. You can use the following or create your own: "Great President Buer, wise healer and teacher of knowledge, I invite you into this sacred space. Guide me with your wisdom, heal me with your touch, and enlighten me with your teachings. I seek to learn from you and honor your presence in my life. Come forth, Buer, and let us commune in harmony."
4. **Meditation and Listening**: After the invocation, sit quietly and meditate. Focus on the sigil and be open to any sensations, thoughts, or messages that come through. Buer may communicate through feelings, visions, or intuitive insights.
5. **Offerings**: It's customary to offer something in return for Buer's guidance. Herbs, wine, or a heartfelt commitment to follow his teachings can be suitable offerings. Place these in your sacred space as a gesture of respect.

Meditative Practices

Meditation is a powerful tool to deepen your connection with Buer. Here are some practices you can incorporate:

1. **Guided Visualization**: Visualize a serene, natural landscape where you meet Buer. Imagine him imparting wisdom and answering your questions. This practice helps build a mental rapport with the spirit.
2. **Breathing Exercises**: Simple breathing exercises can help you attune to Buer's energy. Inhale deeply, hold the breath, and exhale slowly, focusing on your connection to the spirit with each breath.
3. **Mantra Meditation**: Use a mantra or affirmation such as "I am open to Buer's wisdom" during meditation. Repeating this can help align your consciousness with Buer's energy.

Integrating Buer's Teachings

Connecting with Buer is not a one-time event but an ongoing relationship. Here's how to integrate his teachings into your daily life:

1. **Daily Rituals**: Establish daily or weekly rituals to honor Buer and seek his guidance. This can be as simple as lighting a candle and saying a prayer or as elaborate as a full ritual.

2. **Journaling**: Keep a dedicated journal for your experiences with Buer. Document your invocations, meditations, dreams, and any insights you receive. This practice helps solidify your connection and track your spiritual progress.
3. **Applying Knowledge**: Actively apply Buer's teachings to your life. If he imparts knowledge about herbal remedies, integrate them into your health routine. If he offers philosophical insights, reflect on how they can improve your ethical decisions and interactions.

Ethical Considerations

When working with spirits like Buer, it is essential to approach with respect and integrity. Here are some ethical considerations:

1. **Respect and Consent**: Always approach Buer with respect and seek his consent for any guidance or intervention. Treat him as a wise mentor, not as a tool for your desires.

2. **Intentions**: Ensure your intentions are pure and aligned with the greater good. Buer's teachings often emphasize ethical living, so strive to embody these principles in your practice.
3. **Gratitude**: Regularly express gratitude for Buer's presence and teachings. This can be through offerings, prayers, or acts of kindness that honor his influence in your life.

Common Experiences and Challenges

Connecting with a Goetic spirit like Buer can be a profound experience, but it can also come with challenges. Here are some common experiences and how to navigate them:

1. **Initial Silence**: It's not uncommon for initial attempts to connect with Buer to feel unresponsive. Persistence and patience are key. Continue your rituals and meditations with faith and openness.
2. **Overwhelming Energy**: Buer's presence can sometimes feel overwhelming. Grounding techniques, such as walking barefoot on the earth or holding grounding stones like hematite, can help balance the energy.

3. **Doubt and Skepticism**: Doubts are natural, especially when embarking on a spiritual path. Trust your experiences and keep an open mind. Documenting your journey can help affirm the reality of your connection.

Conclusion: A Lifelong Journey

Connecting with Buer is a transformative experience that can enhance your practice of natural magick and enrich your life with wisdom and healing. This relationship is not static but evolves as you grow and deepen your understanding. By committing to this journey with sincerity and respect, you open yourself to a wealth of knowledge and a profound sense of harmony and balance.

In the chapters that follow, we will explore more specific rituals, remedies, and practices guided by Buer's teachings. May your connection with Buer be a source of inspiration, healing, and enlightenment as you continue your path of natural magick.

Chapter 4: Sacred Tools and Spaces

The Power of Preparation

In the world of natural magick, the tools we use and the spaces we create hold profound significance. They are not merely objects and locations but extensions of our intent, conduits for energy, and sanctuaries where the spiritual and physical realms intertwine. Understanding how to craft and maintain your sacred tools and spaces is essential for anyone practicing magick, especially when working with a powerful spirit like Buer.

This chapter will guide you through the process of selecting, consecrating, and using your magickal tools, as well as creating and maintaining sacred spaces that foster a deep connection with Buer. By the end of this chapter, you will have a comprehensive understanding of how to build a foundation for your practice that is both practical and profoundly spiritual.

Selecting Your Sacred Tools

Magickal tools are not just instruments; they are extensions of your will and energy. Each tool has its unique purpose and significance, and choosing the right ones is a personal and intuitive process. Here are some of the essential tools you will need for your practice:

1. **Athame**: The athame is a ritual knife, typically with a double-edged blade. It is used to direct energy, cast circles, and invoke spirits. The athame represents the element of fire or air, depending on your tradition, and is a symbol of your willpower and authority.
2. **Wand**: The wand is another tool for directing energy. It is often made from wood, such as oak, ash, or willow, and can be decorated with crystals, symbols, or personal markings. The wand represents the element of air or fire and is used in rituals involving invocation, healing, and protection.

3. **Pentacle**: The pentacle is a disc inscribed with a pentagram, representing the element of earth. It serves as a protective talisman and a focal point for energy during rituals. The pentacle can be made of various materials, including wood, metal, or clay.
4. **Chalice**: The chalice is a cup used to hold water, wine, or other ritual liquids. It symbolizes the element of water and is associated with the feminine divine, intuition, and emotions. The chalice is used in rituals of purification, healing, and communion.
5. **Incense Burner**: Incense burners hold and burn incense, representing the element of air and the spirit's presence. Incense is used to purify the space, invoke spirits, and enhance the ritual atmosphere.
6. **Candles**: Candles are essential for providing light and representing the element of fire. Different colors of candles are used for various purposes, such as white for purity, green for healing, and blue for communication.

7. **Herbs and Crystals**: Herbs and crystals are powerful allies in natural magick. Each herb and crystal has its unique properties and can be used to enhance rituals, create remedies, and provide protection.

Consecrating Your Tools

Consecrating your tools is a vital step in imbuing them with your personal energy and intent. This process purifies the tools and dedicates them to your magickal work. Here is a simple yet effective consecration ritual:

1. **Cleansing**: Begin by physically cleaning each tool. Use soap and water for items that can be washed, or wipe them down with a cloth. For a deeper energetic cleanse, you can pass each tool through the smoke of purifying herbs like sage or incense.
2. **Circle Casting**: Cast a sacred circle to create a protected space for the consecration ritual. Use your athame or wand to trace the circle in the air, calling upon the elements and spirits to guard and bless the space.
3. **Elemental Blessing**: Consecrate each tool by invoking the four elements:

- **Earth**: Sprinkle a pinch of salt or place the tool on a pentacle, saying, "By the power of earth, I consecrate this [tool] for my sacred work."
- **Air**: Pass the tool through incense smoke, saying, "By the power of air, I consecrate this [tool] for my sacred work."
- **Fire**: Hold the tool over a candle flame (without burning it), saying, "By the power of fire, I consecrate this [tool] for my sacred work."
- **Water**: Sprinkle a few drops of water on the tool, saying, "By the power of water, I consecrate this [tool] for my sacred work."

4. **Spirit Blessing**: Hold the tool to your heart and invoke Buer or another guiding spirit, saying, "Great spirit Buer, I dedicate this [tool] to my sacred practice. May it serve as a vessel of your wisdom and a conduit of healing and harmony."
5. **Closing**: Close the circle by thanking the elements and spirits, and ground any excess energy by touching the earth or a grounding stone.

Creating Sacred Spaces

A sacred space is a sanctuary where the mundane and the magickal meet. It is a place dedicated to your spiritual work, where you can connect with Buer, perform rituals, and find solace. Here's how to create and maintain your sacred space:

1. **Choosing the Location**: Select a space that is quiet, private, and free from distractions. It can be a whole room, a corner of a room, or an outdoor area. Ensure that the space feels comfortable and safe.
2. **Cleansing the Space**: Purify the area using smoke from sage, cedar, or palo santo. Open windows to let in fresh air and natural light. Sprinkle salt or holy water around the perimeter to cleanse and protect the space.
3. **Setting Up an Altar**: An altar is the focal point of your sacred space. It can be a table, shelf, or any flat surface. Decorate your altar with items that hold spiritual significance, such as candles, crystals, statues, and symbols. Include representations of the four elements and a central item to symbolize Buer, such as his sigil or an image.

4. **Personalizing Your Space**: Add personal touches that make the space uniquely yours. This can include artwork, meaningful objects, and items from nature like flowers, leaves, and stones. Your sacred space should reflect your spiritual journey and aspirations.
5. **Maintaining the Space**: Regularly clean and refresh your sacred space to keep the energy vibrant and welcoming. Rearrange items, replace candles and incense, and add seasonal decorations to align with the cycles of nature.

Daily Practices in Your Sacred Space

To deepen your connection with Buer and enhance your practice, incorporate daily rituals and activities in your sacred space:

1. **Morning Rituals**: Begin your day with a simple ritual to set your intentions and align with Buer's energy. Light a candle, say a prayer or affirmation, and spend a few moments in meditation or reflection.
2. **Meditation and Prayer**: Use your sacred space for daily meditation and prayer. Focus on connecting with Buer, seeking his guidance, and expressing gratitude for his presence and teachings.

3. **Journaling**: Keep a journal in your sacred space to record your thoughts, experiences, and insights. Reflect on your rituals, dreams, and any messages you receive from Buer.
4. **Herbal and Crystal Work**: Prepare herbal remedies and crystal grids in your sacred space. Charge your herbs and crystals with specific intentions and use them in your magickal work.
5. **Ritual Baths**: If possible, integrate a ritual bath into your practice. Use herbs, salts, and essential oils in your bath to cleanse and rejuvenate your body and spirit. Perform this ritual in your sacred space if you have a portable basin or nearby bathroom.

Honoring Buer in Your Sacred Space

As you create and use your sacred space, it is important to honor Buer and show gratitude for his guidance:

1. **Offerings**: Regularly place offerings on your altar to honor Buer. These can include herbs, flowers, food, drink, or any items that hold significance. Offerings symbolize your respect and appreciation for his wisdom and assistance.

2. **Rituals of Thanks**: Perform rituals specifically dedicated to thanking Buer. Light candles, recite prayers, and make gestures of gratitude. Expressing thanks strengthens your bond with Buer and reinforces the positive energy in your space.
3. **Seasonal Celebrations**: Celebrate seasonal changes and festivals in your sacred space. Create rituals that align with the natural cycles and honor Buer's connection to the earth and its rhythms.

Conclusion: The Heart of Your Practice

Your sacred tools and spaces are the heart of your magickal practice. They provide the foundation for your rituals, meditations, and connections with Buer. By carefully selecting and consecrating your tools and creating a sacred space that reflects your spiritual journey, you enhance your ability to work effectively and harmoniously in the realm of natural magick.

As you continue your journey with Buer, remember that your sacred space is a living, evolving sanctuary. It grows and changes with you, reflecting your personal growth and spiritual evolution. Nurture it with care, respect, and gratitude, and it will remain a powerful source of inspiration, healing, and transformation in your life.

May your sacred tools serve you well, and may your sacred space be a haven of peace, wisdom, and magick.

Chapter 5: Understanding Herbal Energies

The Life Force Within

In the practice of natural magick, herbs are more than just plants; they are living entities imbued with unique energies and properties that can profoundly influence our lives. Understanding herbal energies is a fundamental aspect of working with natural magick and an essential skill for any practitioner seeking to harness the power of nature. This chapter will delve into the vibrant world of herbal energies, offering insights into their properties, uses, and the ways they can be integrated into your magickal practice.

The Essence of Herbal Energies

Herbal energies are the subtle yet potent forces contained within plants. These energies can be harnessed for healing, protection, empowerment, and spiritual growth. Each herb possesses a distinct energy signature, influenced by its physical properties, growing conditions, and the environment it inhabits. By tuning into these energies, we can align ourselves with the natural world and amplify our magickal intentions.

The ancient practice of herbalism recognizes that every plant has a spirit or essence that embodies its unique characteristics. This essence is what gives herbs their magickal and medicinal properties. For instance, lavender's calming energy can soothe the mind and spirit, while rosemary's protective qualities can ward off negative influences. Understanding these energies allows us to select and use herbs with precision and purpose.

Connecting with Herbal Energies

To effectively work with herbal energies, it is crucial to develop a deep connection with the plants you use. This connection goes beyond mere knowledge of their properties; it involves a spiritual and intuitive bond that enhances your magickal practice. Here are some ways to connect with herbal energies:

1. **Cultivating Plants**: Growing your own herbs is one of the best ways to connect with their energies. Tending to the plants, observing their growth, and harvesting them with care establishes a personal relationship and deepens your understanding of their essence.

2. **Meditation and Visualization**: Spend time meditating with each herb. Hold a sprig or leaf in your hand, close your eyes, and visualize its energy flowing into you. Pay attention to any sensations, images, or messages that arise during this meditation.
3. **Herb Walks**: Take walks in nature to observe and gather wild herbs. Walking mindfully in natural settings helps you attune to the energies of the plants and the environment. Approach this practice with respect and gratitude for the natural world.
4. **Herbal Offerings**: Make offerings to the spirits of the plants you work with. This can be as simple as watering them, placing small tokens of appreciation at their base, or performing a brief ritual of thanks. Offerings build a reciprocal relationship and honor the plants' contributions to your practice.

The Language of Herbal Energies

Each herb communicates its energy through various correspondences, including its appearance, scent, taste, and the elements it is associated with. Understanding these correspondences helps you select the right herbs for your magickal workings. Here are some key correspondences to consider:

1. **Elements**: Herbs are often associated with one or more of the four classical elements (earth, air, fire, water). For example, basil is linked with fire due to its energizing properties, while chamomile is associated with water for its calming and soothing effects.
2. **Planetary Influences**: Many herbs are connected to specific planets, which can enhance their magickal properties. For instance, rosemary is associated with the Sun, symbolizing vitality and protection, while lavender is linked to Mercury, representing communication and peace.

3. **Colors**: The color of an herb or its flowers can indicate its magickal properties. Red herbs like cayenne pepper are often used for courage and strength, while white herbs like sage are used for purification and clarity.
4. **Scent and Taste**: The aroma and flavor of an herb can reveal its energy. Aromatic herbs like mint and eucalyptus are invigorating and refreshing, while sweet herbs like vanilla and cinnamon are comforting and nurturing.

Practical Applications of Herbal Energies

Understanding herbal energies allows you to harness their power in a variety of magickal and healing practices. Here are some practical applications:

1. **Healing and Wellness**: Use herbs to create natural remedies that promote physical, emotional, and spiritual health. For example, a tea made from chamomile and lavender can soothe anxiety and promote restful sleep, while a poultice of comfrey can aid in healing wounds and bruises.

2. **Protection and Cleansing**: Incorporate protective and purifying herbs into your rituals and spells. Burn sage or cedar to cleanse your space of negative energies, or carry a pouch of rosemary and garlic for personal protection.
3. **Empowerment and Attraction**: Enhance your personal power and attract positive influences with the help of herbs. Use cinnamon and ginger in spells to boost confidence and success, or sprinkle rose petals and jasmine in love magick to draw affection and harmony.
4. **Divination and Spiritual Growth**: Use herbs to enhance your psychic abilities and spiritual practices. Mugwort and bay leaves can be used to stimulate prophetic dreams, while frankincense and sandalwood can be burned to deepen meditation and connect with higher realms.

Creating Herbal Blends

Combining herbs into blends amplifies their energies and creates synergistic effects. When creating herbal blends, consider the specific goals of your magickal workings and select herbs that complement each other. Here are some tips for creating effective herbal blends:

1. **Intention Setting**: Clearly define the purpose of your blend. Whether it's for healing, protection, love, or spiritual growth, your intention will guide your selection of herbs.
2. **Balance and Harmony**: Choose herbs that work well together and create a balanced energy. Avoid combining too many herbs with conflicting properties, as this can dilute their effectiveness.
3. **Preparation and Storage**: Prepare your herbal blends with care, using clean tools and containers. Store them in a cool, dark place to preserve their potency. Label each blend with its ingredients and intended use.
4. **Ritual Charging**: Charge your herbal blends with energy by performing a ritual or meditation. Hold the blend in your hands, visualize your intention, and infuse it with your energy and the energy of the elements.

Rituals and Practices with Herbal Energies

Incorporating herbal energies into your rituals and practices enhances their effectiveness and deepens your connection with the natural world. Here are some rituals and practices to try:

1. **Herbal Baths**: Prepare a ritual bath with herbs to cleanse and rejuvenate your body and spirit. Add a sachet of lavender, chamomile, and rose petals to your bathwater, and immerse yourself in the soothing energies of the herbs.
2. **Herbal Incense**: Create your own incense blends using dried herbs and resins. Burn the incense during rituals to purify the space, invoke spirits, or enhance your magickal workings. Popular herbs for incense include sage, rosemary, and frankincense.
3. **Herbal Talismans**: Craft talismans or amulets using herbs to carry their energies with you. Sew small pouches filled with protective herbs like garlic and black salt, or create love charms with rose petals and vanilla beans. Carry these talismans in your pocket or place them under your pillow.

4. **Herbal Offerings**: Offer herbs to the spirits, deities, or elements you work with. Place fresh or dried herbs on your altar, in a sacred space, or in nature as a gesture of gratitude and respect. Offerings can include herbs like thyme for courage, mint for prosperity, or basil for protection.

Developing Your Herbal Practice

As you continue to explore and work with herbal energies, you will develop your own unique practice. Here are some ways to deepen your relationship with herbs and enhance your magickal abilities:

1. **Study and Research**: Continuously educate yourself about herbs and their properties. Read books, attend workshops, and consult reputable sources to expand your knowledge. Experiment with different herbs and blends to discover what works best for you.
2. **Record Your Experiences**: Keep a journal of your herbal practices, noting the herbs you use, their effects, and any insights or messages you receive. This record will help you track your progress and refine your techniques.

3. **Build a Herbal Garden**: If possible, cultivate a garden with the herbs you frequently use. Growing your own herbs provides a fresh and sustainable source of magickal ingredients and deepens your connection to the plants and their energies.
4. **Share Your Knowledge**: Share your herbal knowledge and experiences with others. Teaching and discussing herbal magick with fellow practitioners fosters a sense of community and enriches your own practice.

Conclusion: The Wisdom of Herbs

Understanding herbal energies is a journey of discovery, intuition, and connection with the natural world. By tuning into the unique properties and spirits of herbs, you unlock their magickal potential and bring their healing energies into your life. This knowledge, rooted in ancient traditions and enhanced by personal experience, empowers you to create effective remedies, rituals, and spells that promote health, protection, and spiritual growth.

As you continue to explore the world of herbal magick, remember that each herb is a teacher and ally, offering its wisdom and energy to those who seek it with respect and gratitude. Embrace the journey with an open heart and a curious mind, and you will find that the path of herbal magick leads to profound transformation and harmony.

Chapter 6: Herbal Preparations and Potions

The Alchemy of Nature

Herbs, with their rich history and potent energies, form the backbone of many magickal practices. When prepared and combined with intention, they can create powerful potions and remedies that address physical ailments, emotional needs, and spiritual aspirations. In this chapter, we will explore the art of herbal preparations and potions, guiding you through the processes of crafting these natural elixirs and harnessing their magickal properties.

The Basics of Herbal Preparations

Before diving into the specifics of potion-making, it's essential to understand the fundamental types of herbal preparations. Each method extracts and preserves the beneficial properties of herbs in different ways, allowing for various applications:

1. **Infusions**: Similar to making tea, infusions are created by steeping herbs in hot water. This method is ideal for extracting the delicate essences of leaves and flowers. Infusions are typically used for medicinal teas, baths, and washes.

2. **Decoctions**: Decoctions involve simmering tougher plant materials, such as roots, bark, and seeds, in water. This method extracts more resilient compounds and is often used for more potent medicinal brews and magickal potions.
3. **Tinctures**: Tinctures are made by soaking herbs in alcohol or vinegar. This process extracts and preserves the active ingredients, resulting in a highly concentrated form that can be stored for long periods. Tinctures are taken in small doses and used in both healing and magickal applications.
4. **Oils**: Herbal oils are created by infusing herbs in a carrier oil, such as olive or coconut oil. This method extracts the fat-soluble compounds and is used for anointing, massage, and skin care.
5. **Salves and Balms**: These are semi-solid preparations made by combining herbal oils with beeswax or other natural thickeners. Salves and balms are used topically to soothe and heal the skin.

6. **Syrups**: Herbal syrups are made by combining decoctions or infusions with honey or sugar, creating a sweet and palatable remedy. They are commonly used for treating coughs and sore throats.
7. **Poultices and Compresses**: These preparations involve applying fresh or dried herbs directly to the skin. Poultices use whole herbs, while compresses are soaked in herbal infusions or decoctions. Both are used for localized healing.

Gathering and Preparing Herbs

The quality and potency of your herbal preparations depend on the herbs you use. Whether you grow your own, forage in the wild, or purchase from reputable sources, it's crucial to ensure they are fresh, high-quality, and free from contaminants. Here are some tips for gathering and preparing herbs:

1. **Harvesting**: When harvesting herbs, do so with respect and gratitude. Choose a dry, sunny day, and gather herbs in the morning after the dew has evaporated. Use sharp scissors or a knife to avoid damaging the plants. Harvest only what you need and leave enough for the plant to continue thriving.

2. **Drying**: Drying herbs preserves their potency for future use. Bundle small bunches of herbs and hang them upside down in a warm, dark, well-ventilated space. Alternatively, use a dehydrator or an oven set to a low temperature. Once dried, store the herbs in airtight containers away from light and moisture.
3. **Storage**: Proper storage ensures your herbs retain their potency. Use glass jars or metal tins with tight-fitting lids. Label each container with the name of the herb and the date of harvest. Store in a cool, dark place.

Crafting Potions

Potion-making is an art that combines intention, knowledge, and creativity. Each potion is a unique blend of herbs, energies, and magickal intent, crafted to address specific needs or desires. Here are some foundational steps to guide you in crafting your potions:

1. **Setting Intentions**: The first step in potion-making is setting a clear intention. What do you want to achieve with your potion? Whether it's healing, protection, love, or spiritual insight, your intention will guide your choice of herbs and the overall preparation process.
2. **Selecting Herbs**: Choose herbs that align with your intention. Research their properties and correspondences to ensure they complement each other and enhance the desired effect. For example, lavender and chamomile for calming potions, or rosemary and thyme for protective brews.
3. **Charging and Blessing**: Before preparing your potion, charge and bless the herbs. Hold them in your hands, visualize your intention, and infuse them with your energy. You can also use a blessing chant or prayer to enhance their potency.
4. **Combining Ingredients**: Follow the appropriate method for your potion, whether it's an infusion, decoction, tincture, or another preparation. Combine the herbs with intention, focusing on the energy you wish to imbue into the potion.

5. **Ritual Preparation**: Perform the preparation as a ritual, in a sacred space, and at a time that aligns with your intention. For example, creating a love potion during a waxing moon or a protection potion on a Saturday.
6. **Storage and Use**: Once prepared, store your potion in a dark glass bottle, preferably with a tight-fitting lid. Label it with the name, ingredients, and date. Use your potion as needed, with respect and gratitude for the herbs and the energies involved.

Practical Recipes

Here are some practical potion recipes to get you started on your journey:

1. **Calming Tea**: Combine equal parts of dried chamomile, lavender, and lemon balm. Steep 1-2 teaspoons in a cup of hot water for 5-10 minutes. Drink to soothe anxiety and promote relaxation.

2. **Healing Tincture**: Fill a glass jar halfway with dried echinacea root, elderberries, and ginger root. Cover with vodka or apple cider vinegar, ensuring the herbs are fully submerged. Seal the jar and let it sit in a dark, cool place for 4-6 weeks, shaking it occasionally. Strain and bottle the tincture. Take 1-2 dropperfuls daily to boost the immune system.
3. **Protection Oil**: Fill a small jar with dried rosemary, sage, and thyme. Cover with olive oil and let it infuse for 2-4 weeks in a warm, dark place. Strain and store the oil in a dark glass bottle. Use to anoint candles, doors, and windows for protection.
4. **Love Syrup**: Combine 1 cup of rose petals, 1 cup of hibiscus flowers, and 1 cinnamon stick in a saucepan with 2 cups of water. Simmer for 20 minutes, then strain. Add 1 cup of honey and stir until dissolved. Bottle and take 1-2 teaspoons daily to attract love and harmony.

5. **Dream Poultice**: Mix dried mugwort, bay leaves, and lavender with a little water to create a paste. Apply to a cloth and place it on your forehead before sleep to enhance dreams and promote prophetic visions.

Ethical Considerations

Working with herbs requires a respectful and ethical approach. Here are some considerations to keep in mind:

1. **Sustainability**: Harvest herbs sustainably, taking only what you need and leaving enough for the plant to continue growing. Support ethical suppliers who practice sustainable farming and wildcrafting.
2. **Respect for Nature**: Approach your herbal work with gratitude and respect for the natural world. Offer thanks to the plants and the earth for their gifts.
3. **Personal Responsibility**: Use herbal preparations responsibly. Be aware of any potential allergies, interactions with medications, or contraindications. If in doubt, consult with a qualified herbalist or healthcare provider.

Conclusion: The Magick of Herbal Preparations

Herbal preparations and potions are a bridge between the physical and the magickal, offering tangible ways to harness the energies of the natural world. By mastering the art of potion-making, you can create powerful remedies and elixirs that support your health, protect your space, attract positive influences, and deepen your spiritual practice.

As you continue your journey with herbal magick, remember that each preparation is a unique expression of your intent and creativity. Approach the process with reverence, curiosity, and a willingness to learn, and you will find that the art of crafting herbal preparations and potions becomes a deeply rewarding and transformative practice.

May your herbal brews be potent, your intentions pure, and your magickal journey ever enriching.

Chapter 7: Healing with Herbs

The Ancient Art of Herbal Healing

Since the dawn of human civilization, herbs have played a crucial role in healing and wellness. Across cultures and continents, our ancestors turned to the natural world for remedies to soothe ailments, restore balance, and promote overall well-being. Today, the ancient art of herbal healing continues to thrive, offering a powerful and holistic approach to health. This chapter will explore the principles and practices of healing with herbs, guiding you through the journey of integrating these natural allies into your life for physical, emotional, and spiritual health.

Understanding Herbal Healing

Herbal healing is based on the principle that plants contain natural compounds that can support and enhance the body's innate ability to heal. Unlike synthetic medications that often target specific symptoms, herbs work holistically, addressing the underlying causes of illness and promoting balance within the body. This approach aligns with the natural rhythms of the body and supports its intrinsic healing processes.

Each herb has its own unique set of properties and actions. Some herbs are known for their anti-inflammatory effects, others for their ability to calm the nervous system or boost the immune response. By understanding these properties, you can choose the right herbs to support your health and address specific conditions.

The Wisdom of Tradition

The practice of herbal healing is steeped in tradition. Ancient cultures from China to Egypt, India to the Americas, developed sophisticated systems of herbal medicine, many of which form the foundation of modern herbal practices. Traditional Chinese Medicine (TCM), Ayurveda, Native American herbalism, and European folk medicine all offer rich repositories of knowledge, passed down through generations.

Learning from these traditions can deepen your understanding of herbal healing. TCM, for instance, classifies herbs based on their energetic properties, such as warming or cooling, and their effects on the body's meridians. Ayurveda considers the doshas—Vata, Pitta, and Kapha—and uses herbs to balance these fundamental energies. By studying these systems, you can gain insights into how different herbs can be used to restore harmony and health.

The Power of Common Herbs

While there are thousands of herbs with medicinal properties, some stand out for their versatility and effectiveness. Here are a few common herbs that you can incorporate into your healing practice:

1. **Chamomile (Matricaria chamomilla)**: Known for its calming and anti-inflammatory properties, chamomile is excellent for soothing digestive issues, reducing anxiety, and promoting restful sleep.
2. **Echinacea (Echinacea purpurea)**: A powerful immune booster, echinacea is often used to prevent and treat colds and flu. It also has anti-inflammatory and wound-healing properties.

3. **Ginger (Zingiber officinale)**: Ginger is renowned for its ability to alleviate nausea, improve digestion, and reduce inflammation. It's also effective in warming the body and enhancing circulation.
4. **Lavender (Lavandula angustifolia)**: Lavender's calming and soothing effects make it a popular choice for reducing stress, anxiety, and insomnia. It also has antiseptic and anti-inflammatory properties.
5. **Peppermint (Mentha × piperita)**: Peppermint is commonly used to relieve digestive discomfort, reduce headaches, and improve respiratory function. Its cooling and refreshing properties make it a versatile herb for various ailments.
6. **Turmeric (Curcuma longa)**: Turmeric is celebrated for its anti-inflammatory and antioxidant properties. It's used to support joint health, improve digestion, and enhance liver function.

Preparing Herbal Remedies

Creating your own herbal remedies is a deeply rewarding process that connects you directly with the healing power of plants. Here are some simple yet effective methods for preparing herbal remedies:

1. **Herbal Teas and Infusions**: One of the simplest ways to use herbs is to make teas and infusions. Pour boiling water over the herbs, cover, and let steep for 10-15 minutes. Strain and drink. This method is ideal for delicate parts of the plant, such as leaves and flowers.
2. **Herbal Tinctures**: Tinctures are concentrated herbal extracts made by soaking herbs in alcohol or vinegar. Fill a jar with dried or fresh herbs, cover with alcohol (like vodka) or apple cider vinegar, and let sit for 4-6 weeks, shaking occasionally. Strain and bottle. Tinctures are taken in small doses, usually diluted in water.

3. **Herbal Oils and Salves**: Infuse herbs in a carrier oil (such as olive or coconut oil) for several weeks. Strain the oil and use it as is, or combine it with beeswax to create a salve. These preparations are excellent for topical use to soothe skin conditions, relieve pain, and promote healing.
4. **Herbal Syrups**: Make a strong decoction of herbs by simmering them in water. Strain and add honey or sugar to create a syrup. This method is particularly useful for soothing coughs and sore throats.

Integrating Herbs into Daily Life

To fully benefit from the healing power of herbs, it's essential to integrate them into your daily routine. Here are some practical ways to incorporate herbs into your everyday life:

1. **Herbal Morning Routine**: Start your day with an herbal tea that suits your needs. For example, drink a cup of ginger tea to boost digestion and energy, or chamomile tea to start the day calmly.

2. **Cooking with Herbs**: Use culinary herbs like basil, oregano, thyme, and rosemary in your cooking. These herbs not only enhance the flavor of your meals but also provide numerous health benefits.
3. **Herbal Baths**: Add dried herbs or a few drops of essential oils to your bath for a relaxing and therapeutic experience. Lavender and chamomile are excellent choices for a calming bath, while peppermint and eucalyptus can invigorate and refresh.
4. **Herbal Compresses**: Use herbal infusions or decoctions to make warm or cold compresses. Apply these compresses to sore muscles, bruises, or areas of inflammation to reduce pain and promote healing.
5. **Herbal Inhalation**: Inhale the steam from a pot of boiling water with added herbs like eucalyptus, peppermint, or thyme to clear congestion and improve respiratory function.

The Mind-Body-Spirit Connection
Herbal healing is not just about addressing physical symptoms; it's about nurturing the whole person—body, mind, and spirit. Herbs can play a significant role in supporting mental and emotional health. For instance, herbs like lavender, lemon balm, and valerian can help reduce anxiety and promote relaxation.

Adaptogenic herbs like ashwagandha and holy basil support the body in managing stress and maintaining balance. Spiritually, herbs can enhance your magickal practices and deepen your connection to the natural world. Use herbs in rituals, meditations, and as offerings to spirits and deities. Burn sage or palo santo to cleanse your space and invite positive energies. Incorporate herbs like mugwort and yarrow into your divination practices to enhance intuition and clarity.

Working with a Herbal Mentor

While self-study and experimentation are valuable, working with a knowledgeable herbal mentor can significantly enhance your practice. A mentor can provide guidance, share wisdom from their own experiences, and help you navigate the complexities of herbal healing. Seek out local herbalists, join herbal study groups, or enroll in online courses to deepen your knowledge and skills.

Ethical and Sustainable Practices

As you engage in herbal healing, it's important to practice sustainably and ethically. Harvest herbs responsibly, ensuring you do not over-harvest or damage wild populations. Support organic and sustainable growers, and be mindful of the environmental impact of your herbal practices. Respect the plants and the ecosystems they come from, offering gratitude and reciprocity for their gifts.

Conclusion: A Journey of Healing

Healing with herbs is a journey of discovery, empowerment, and connection. By integrating herbs into your life, you can enhance your health, deepen your magickal practice, and cultivate a profound relationship with the natural world. Remember that herbal healing is a dynamic and evolving practice. Stay curious, continue learning, and remain open to the wisdom that the plants have to offer.

May the healing energies of herbs guide you toward greater well-being, balance, and harmony in all aspects of your life. Embrace the ancient art of herbal healing, and let it be a source of strength, comfort, and transformation on your path.

Chapter 8: Magical Herb Gardens

Cultivating Your Personal Sanctuary

Imagine stepping into a garden where each plant is chosen with intention, each herb holds a story, and every leaf, flower, and root resonates with magickal energy. A magical herb garden is more than just a collection of plants; it is a living sanctuary where nature's power intertwines with your personal magickal practice. In this chapter, we will explore the art and joy of creating your own magical herb garden, guiding you through the steps of planning, planting, and nurturing a space that will enhance your magickal workings and bring harmony and healing into your life.

The Vision of a Magical Herb Garden

A magical herb garden is a space designed with both practical and spiritual purposes in mind. It is a place where you can grow the herbs you need for your magickal and healing practices, and also a sanctuary where you can connect with the natural world, meditate, and perform rituals. The process of creating and tending this garden is itself a deeply rewarding and transformative practice.

The vision for your magical herb garden should reflect your personal goals and intentions. Do you want a tranquil space for meditation and reflection? A vibrant garden filled with herbs for spellwork and healing? Or perhaps a combination of both? Whatever your vision, the key is to infuse the garden with your magickal intent and make it a true extension of your spiritual practice.

Planning Your Garden

Planning is a crucial step in creating a successful magical herb garden. Consider the following aspects when designing your garden:

1. **Location**: Choose a location that receives adequate sunlight, as most herbs thrive in full sun. Ensure the area has good soil drainage and is easily accessible for regular tending. If you have limited outdoor space, consider container gardening or creating a small indoor herb garden.

2. **Layout and Design**: Decide on the layout of your garden. You might want to arrange your herbs in circular patterns to represent the cycles of nature, or in sections based on their magickal correspondences (such as healing, protection, love, etc.). Incorporate pathways, seating areas, and focal points like a central altar or statue to enhance the garden's magickal ambiance.
3. **Herb Selection**: Choose herbs that align with your magickal and healing needs. Research the growing requirements and magickal properties of each herb. Consider incorporating a mix of perennial and annual herbs to ensure year-round interest and availability.
4. **Elements and Symbolism**: Integrate elements and symbols that enhance the magickal energy of your garden. Use stones, crystals, wind chimes, water features, and statues of deities or spirits to create a sacred atmosphere. These elements can also serve as focal points for meditation and ritual.

Planting with Intention

Once you have planned your garden, it's time to bring it to life by planting with intention. The act of planting is a powerful ritual in itself, symbolizing growth, transformation, and the manifestation of your desires.

1. **Preparation**: Prepare the soil by clearing any debris and enriching it with compost or organic matter. As you work the soil, infuse it with your energy and intention. Visualize your garden flourishing and radiating with magickal power.
2. **Blessing the Seeds and Plants**: Before planting, bless the seeds and young plants. Hold them in your hands, and speak words of blessing and intention. You might say something like, "I bless you with the energy of growth and magick. May you thrive and bring healing, protection, and wisdom into this garden."

3. **Planting Ritual**: Plant each herb with care, following the spacing and depth requirements for each type. As you place each plant in the ground, say a short invocation or prayer, connecting the herb with its magickal purpose. For example, when planting rosemary, you might say, "Rosemary, I plant you for protection and remembrance. May your energy guard this space and bring clarity to my mind."
4. **Watering and Nurturing**: Water the newly planted herbs thoroughly and continue to care for them with regular watering, weeding, and pruning. As you tend to your garden, infuse each action with love and intention. This ongoing care strengthens your connection to the herbs and enhances their magickal potency.

Harvesting with Respect

Harvesting herbs from your magical garden is a sacred act that should be done with respect and gratitude. The way you gather your herbs can significantly impact their magickal energy.

1. **Timing**: Harvest herbs at the optimal time for their intended use. For most herbs, this means in the morning after the dew has dried but before the heat of the day. Magickally, certain times of the moon cycle (such as the full moon for abundance or the waning moon for banishing) can enhance the properties of the herbs.
2. **Gratitude and Offerings**: Before harvesting, offer thanks to the plant and the spirit of the herb. You can leave a small offering, such as a pinch of tobacco, a crystal, or a prayer of gratitude. Ask for permission and express your appreciation for the herb's gifts.
3. **Harvesting Method**: Use clean, sharp scissors or a knife to cut the herbs, making clean cuts to avoid damaging the plant. Harvest only what you need, and never take more than one-third of the plant at a time to ensure it continues to grow and thrive.

4. **Processing and Storage**: Dry the harvested herbs by hanging them in small bundles in a dark, airy space, or use a dehydrator. Once dried, store the herbs in airtight containers away from light and moisture. Label each container with the herb's name and the date of harvest.

Integrating Your Garden into Magickal Practice

Your magical herb garden is a living part of your spiritual practice. Here are some ways to integrate it into your magickal workings:

1. **Meditation and Reflection**: Spend time meditating in your garden. Sit quietly, listen to the sounds of nature, and connect with the energies of the plants. Use this time for reflection, grounding, and receiving intuitive insights.
2. **Rituals and Spells**: Use your garden as a sacred space for rituals and spellwork. Create a small altar with stones, candles, and offerings. Incorporate fresh herbs into your spells for added potency. For example, use basil leaves in a prosperity spell or sage in a purification ritual.

3. **Herbal Crafts**: Craft herbal charms, sachets, and amulets using herbs from your garden. These items can be used for protection, love, healing, and other magickal purposes. The act of crafting with intention further empowers the herbs and the items you create.
4. **Seasonal Celebrations**: Celebrate the cycles of nature and the changing seasons in your garden. Decorate your space for Sabbats and Esbats, and perform seasonal rituals that honor the earth's rhythms. Planting and harvesting rituals, in particular, align you with the cycles of growth and transformation.

The Ongoing Journey

Creating and tending a magical herb garden is an ongoing journey of growth, learning, and transformation. It requires patience, dedication, and a deep connection to the natural world. As you work with your garden, you will develop a profound relationship with the herbs and the energies they embody.

Remember that a magical herb garden is a living, evolving entity. It reflects the cycles of nature, the ebb and flow of life, and your personal journey. Embrace the process with an open heart and a willingness to learn from the plants and the earth.

Conclusion: A Garden of Magick and Healing

A magical herb garden is more than just a space filled with plants; it is a sanctuary where magick, nature, and personal intention come together to create a powerful source of healing and transformation. By cultivating your own magical herb garden, you create a living testament to your commitment to natural magick and the wisdom of the earth.

As you continue to tend and nurture your garden, may it bring you endless joy, peace, and magickal inspiration. Let each plant be a reminder of the profound connection you share with the natural world and the limitless potential for growth and healing that lies within you. May your magical herb garden flourish and thrive, and may it always be a source of beauty, wisdom, and magick in your life.

Chapter 9: Daily Rituals for Well-being

The Power of Daily Rituals

In our fast-paced, modern world, it's easy to lose sight of the small moments that ground us and bring balance to our lives. Daily rituals serve as touchstones that help us reconnect with our inner selves, align with our intentions, and cultivate a sense of well-being. These rituals are not grand or elaborate; rather, they are simple practices that, when performed regularly, can transform our physical, emotional, and spiritual health. In this chapter, we will explore the art of creating and maintaining daily rituals that enhance your well-being and infuse your life with magick and intention.

The Importance of Consistency

The key to effective daily rituals is consistency. By committing to regular practices, you create a rhythm and structure that support your overall well-being. These rituals become anchors in your day, providing moments of calm, focus, and reflection. Over time, they help to build resilience, reduce stress, and foster a deeper connection to your inner self and the natural world.

Consistency doesn't mean rigidity. Life is dynamic, and flexibility is essential. The goal is to integrate these rituals into your daily routine in a way that feels natural and sustainable. Start with one or two simple practices and gradually build from there, allowing each ritual to become a cherished part of your day.

Morning Rituals: Setting the Tone for the Day

Morning rituals set the tone for your day, helping you to begin with clarity, intention, and positivity. Here are some ideas for creating a powerful morning ritual:

1. **Gratitude Practice**: Begin your day by listing three things you are grateful for. This practice shifts your mindset to one of abundance and positivity. Write them down in a journal or simply reflect on them as you wake up.
2. **Morning Meditation**: Spend a few minutes in quiet meditation. Focus on your breath, set your intention for the day, and visualize your goals. This practice helps to center your mind and prepare you for the challenges ahead.

3. **Sun Salutation**: If you enjoy physical activity, perform a few rounds of sun salutations. This series of yoga poses energizes the body, improves flexibility, and connects you with the natural rhythm of the day.
4. **Herbal Tea Ritual**: Prepare a cup of herbal tea using herbs that align with your intentions for the day. For example, drink peppermint tea for focus and clarity, or chamomile tea for calm and relaxation. As you sip your tea, visualize the energy of the herbs infusing your body and mind.

Midday Rituals: Recharging and Rebalancing

Midday rituals provide an opportunity to pause, recharge, and rebalance. These practices help to break up the day and maintain your energy and focus:

1. **Mindful Breaks**: Take short, mindful breaks throughout your day. Step outside, take a few deep breaths, and reconnect with the natural world. This practice helps to clear your mind and reduce stress.

2. **Energy-Boosting Snacks**: Choose snacks that nourish your body and mind. Fresh fruits, nuts, and seeds provide sustained energy and vital nutrients. Avoid processed foods that can lead to energy crashes.
3. **Stretch and Move**: Incorporate gentle stretches or a brief walk into your midday routine. Movement helps to release tension, improve circulation, and boost your mood.
4. **Aromatherapy**: Use essential oils to enhance your focus and well-being. Diffuse oils like rosemary for concentration, or lavender for relaxation. You can also apply diluted essential oils to your pulse points for a quick pick-me-up.

Evening Rituals: Unwinding and Reflecting

Evening rituals help to unwind from the day's activities and prepare for restful sleep. These practices promote relaxation, reflection, and a sense of closure:

1. **Digital Detox**: Disconnect from electronic devices at least an hour before bed. The blue light from screens can interfere with your sleep cycle. Use this time for more calming activities.

2. **Journaling**: Spend a few minutes journaling about your day. Reflect on your accomplishments, challenges, and moments of joy. This practice helps to process your thoughts and emotions, providing clarity and insight.
3. **Herbal Bath**: Take a relaxing herbal bath with lavender, chamomile, or Epsom salts. The warm water and soothing herbs help to relax your muscles and calm your mind, preparing you for a good night's sleep.
4. **Bedtime Meditation**: End your day with a short meditation or mindfulness practice. Focus on your breath, release any lingering tension, and visualize a peaceful, restorative sleep. This practice helps to quiet your mind and promote deep relaxation.

Integrating Magick into Daily Rituals

Daily rituals provide a perfect opportunity to integrate magick into your routine. By infusing your practices with intention and symbolic actions, you can enhance their effectiveness and deepen your spiritual connection:

1. **Affirmations and Intentions**: Begin each day with affirmations that align with your goals and intentions. Speak them aloud or write them down, visualizing them manifesting in your life. For example, "I am confident and capable," or "I attract positive energy and opportunities."
2. **Elemental Invocations**: Incorporate the elements into your rituals. Light a candle to invoke the element of fire, sprinkle water to represent water, use crystals for earth, and burn incense for air. These actions create a sacred space and enhance your magickal practice.
3. **Lunar Alignments**: Align your rituals with the phases of the moon. Perform rituals for new beginnings during the new moon, set intentions during the waxing moon, celebrate achievements during the full moon, and release negativity during the waning moon. This alignment with lunar cycles amplifies your intentions and connects you with natural rhythms.

4. **Nature Connection**: Spend time in nature as part of your daily rituals. Walk barefoot on the grass, sit under a tree, or simply observe the natural world around you. This practice grounds your energy and strengthens your connection to the earth.

Creating Personalized Rituals

The most effective daily rituals are those that resonate with your unique needs and preferences. Here are some tips for creating personalized rituals that support your well-being:

1. **Identify Your Needs**: Reflect on what you need most in your daily life. Do you need more energy, focus, relaxation, or balance? Tailor your rituals to address these specific needs.
2. **Keep It Simple**: Start with simple practices that are easy to incorporate into your routine. As you become more comfortable, you can add more elements or extend the time spent on each ritual.

3. **Make It Sacred**: Treat your rituals as sacred time for yourself. Create a designated space for your practices, free from distractions. Use tools and symbols that hold personal significance and enhance the sacredness of the moment.
4. **Stay Flexible**: Allow your rituals to evolve as your needs and circumstances change. Be open to trying new practices and adjusting your routine to maintain its relevance and effectiveness.

The Benefits of Daily Rituals

Incorporating daily rituals into your life offers numerous benefits for your physical, emotional, and spiritual well-being:

1. **Stress Reduction**: Regular rituals provide moments of calm and reflection, helping to reduce stress and anxiety. They create a sense of routine and stability, which can be particularly comforting during times of uncertainty.

2. **Improved Focus and Productivity**: Starting your day with intention-setting rituals enhances your focus and productivity. Midday rituals help to maintain your energy and prevent burnout, while evening rituals promote restful sleep and recovery.
3. **Enhanced Well-being**: Daily rituals support your overall well-being by promoting healthy habits, nurturing your mind and body, and fostering a deeper connection with your inner self and the natural world.
4. **Spiritual Growth**: Integrating magickal practices into your daily rituals deepens your spiritual connection and enhances your magickal abilities. It creates a continuous flow of energy and intention that supports your spiritual growth and transformation.

Conclusion: A Life Enriched by Rituals

Daily rituals are powerful tools for enhancing well-being and infusing your life with magick and intention. By creating and maintaining these practices, you cultivate a sense of balance, clarity, and connection that supports your physical, emotional, and spiritual health.

As you continue to develop your daily rituals, remember that the most important aspect is consistency and intention. Approach each practice with an open heart and a mindful presence, allowing the benefits to unfold naturally over time.

May your daily rituals bring you peace, joy, and transformation, and may they serve as a constant reminder of the magick that flows through every moment of your life. Embrace the power of daily rituals and let them guide you on your path to well-being and spiritual fulfillment.

Chapter 10: Cleansing and Purification

The Necessity of Cleansing and Purification

In the practice of natural magick, cleansing and purification are foundational. These acts are essential to maintaining a clear, focused, and powerful spiritual practice. Whether we are dealing with the energies in our homes, our personal auras, or the tools we use in rituals, regular cleansing and purification ensure that we are working with pure, undisturbed energies. This chapter will delve into the methods and importance of cleansing and purification, helping you to keep your magickal practice vibrant and effective.

Understanding Energetic Cleanliness
Just as physical spaces gather dust and dirt, energetic spaces can accumulate unwanted and negative energies. These energies can stem from various sources, including stressful events, negative emotions, and interactions with other people. Over time, these energies can build up, creating a stagnant or even harmful environment. Cleansing and purification help to remove these unwanted energies, restoring balance and harmony.

Energetic cleanliness is not just about the absence of negative energy; it's also about creating a space filled with positive, uplifting vibrations. When we cleanse and purify, we make room for new, beneficial energies to flow in, enhancing our magickal work and overall well-being.

The Importance of Regular Practice

Just as you wouldn't clean your home once and expect it to stay that way forever, cleansing and purification are ongoing practices. Regularly engaging in these rituals keeps your energy field and spaces clear, preventing the buildup of negativity and maintaining a high vibrational environment. Establishing a routine for cleansing and purification ensures that your magickal practice remains potent and your personal energy stays vibrant and healthy.

Methods of Cleansing and Purification

There are numerous methods for cleansing and purification, each with its own strengths and applications. Here are some of the most effective and widely used techniques:

1. **Smoke Cleansing**: One of the oldest and most effective methods of cleansing involves using the smoke of sacred herbs. Sage, cedar, sweetgrass, and palo santo are popular choices. Light the herb and let the smoke waft through the space, focusing on areas that feel particularly heavy or stagnant. As the smoke fills the space, visualize it absorbing and carrying away all negative energies.

2. **Salt Cleansing**: Salt is a powerful purifier, capable of absorbing negative energy. Sprinkle salt around the perimeter of your space, in the corners of rooms, or create a line of salt at doorways and windowsills to prevent negative energy from entering. You can also take a salt bath, adding a handful of sea salt or Epsom salt to the water to cleanse your aura.
3. **Sound Cleansing**: Sound can break up and disperse negative energies effectively. Use bells, chimes, singing bowls, or even clapping your hands to cleanse a space. Walk through the area, making sound, and visualize the vibrations shattering and dissipating any unwanted energies.
4. **Water Cleansing**: Water is a universal purifier. Use a bowl of water infused with cleansing herbs, such as rosemary or lavender, to sprinkle around your space. You can also create a cleansing spray by adding essential oils to water and misting it around the area. Baths and showers are excellent for personal cleansing, especially when combined with sea salt or herbs.

5. **Crystals**: Certain crystals, such as clear quartz, selenite, and black tourmaline, have powerful cleansing properties. Place these crystals in your space or use them to cleanse your tools and personal energy. Selenite wands can be used to "comb" through your aura, removing any negative attachments.
6. **Visualization**: Your mind is a powerful tool for cleansing and purification. Sit quietly, close your eyes, and visualize a brilliant white or golden light filling your space or surrounding your body. See this light dissolving all negative energies, leaving behind only purity and positivity.

Cleansing Your Space

Your home or sacred space is where you conduct your magickal work, meditate, and recharge. Keeping this space energetically clean is crucial for maintaining a harmonious environment:

1. **Regular Maintenance**: Make cleansing a regular part of your routine. Weekly or monthly smoke cleansing, salt sprinkling, or sound cleansing can keep energies from stagnating.

2. **Intentional Focus**: Pay attention to areas that feel particularly heavy or stagnant. These might be corners, closets, or rooms that are rarely used. Spend extra time cleansing these areas, visualizing them being filled with light and positive energy.
3. **Decluttering**: Physical clutter can contribute to energetic clutter. Regularly declutter your space, removing items that no longer serve you. As you do so, visualize negative energies leaving with the clutter.
4. **Blessing and Protection**: After cleansing, bless your space with positive energy. Use incense, essential oils, or flowers to infuse the area with uplifting vibrations. Set up protective wards, such as crystals, amulets, or salt lines, to keep the space clear of future negativity.

Cleansing Your Tools

The tools you use in your magickal practice, such as crystals, wands, and tarot cards, also need regular cleansing. Here's how to keep them energetically pristine:

1. **Smoke Cleansing**: Pass your tools through the smoke of sage, cedar, or palo santo. Visualize the smoke carrying away any residual energies.
2. **Salt**: Place your tools in a bowl of salt or bury them in salt for a few hours. The salt will absorb any negative energies. Be cautious with delicate items, as salt can be abrasive.
3. **Water**: Rinse your tools in a bowl of water infused with cleansing herbs. For items that shouldn't get wet, use a spray bottle to mist them lightly.
4. **Sunlight and Moonlight**: Place your tools in direct sunlight or moonlight to cleanse and recharge them. The light purifies and revitalizes their energy.
5. **Crystal Cleansing**: Place your tools on or near cleansing crystals like selenite or clear quartz. These crystals will absorb and neutralize any unwanted energies.

Personal Cleansing and Purification
Your own energy field, or aura, can accumulate negative energies from daily interactions and experiences. Regular personal cleansing is essential for maintaining your spiritual health:

1. **Daily Cleansing**: Incorporate daily cleansing rituals into your routine. This can be as simple as a quick visualization of white light surrounding you or a short smoke cleansing with sage or palo santo.
2. **Bathing**: Regular baths with sea salt, Epsom salt, or cleansing herbs can help remove negative energies from your aura. Visualize the water washing away any negativity and leaving you refreshed and purified.
3. **Breathwork**: Use deep, intentional breathing to cleanse your energy field. Inhale deeply, visualizing clean, bright energy filling your body, and exhale, releasing any negative or stagnant energy.
4. **Energy Work**: Practice energy work techniques like Reiki, chakra balancing, or aura cleansing to maintain your energetic health. These practices help to clear blockages and ensure a smooth flow of energy through your body.

Combining Methods
Combining multiple cleansing and purification methods can enhance their effectiveness. For example, you might start with a physical decluttering and cleaning, followed by smoke cleansing and sound cleansing. Finish with a visualization or a protective ritual to seal in the positive energy. Experiment with different combinations to find what works best for you and your space.

Conclusion: A Clean Slate for Magick
Cleansing and purification are vital practices for maintaining the energetic health of your space, tools, and personal aura. By regularly engaging in these rituals, you ensure that your magickal work is conducted in a clear, focused, and potent environment. This foundation of cleanliness and purity enhances your ability to manifest your intentions and connect with higher energies.

Embrace the power of cleansing and purification, making it a regular and cherished part of your spiritual practice. As you do so, you will find that your magick flows more smoothly, your spaces feel more harmonious, and your personal energy remains vibrant and resilient.

May your journey with cleansing and purification bring you clarity, balance, and a deep sense of connection to the purest energies of the universe.

Chapter 11: Protection and Shielding

The Vital Need for Protection

In the practice of natural magick, protection and shielding are essential. As practitioners, we often work with powerful energies and forces, some of which can be overwhelming or even harmful if not properly managed. Protection and shielding rituals create a safe space for our magickal work, safeguarding us from negative influences and ensuring that our spiritual practices are conducted in a harmonious and secure environment. In this chapter, we will explore various methods of protection and shielding, providing you with the tools and knowledge to create strong, effective barriers that guard against unwanted energies.

Understanding Protection and Shielding

Protection in magick is about creating boundaries that keep harmful energies at bay while allowing positive energies to flow freely. Shielding, on the other hand, involves creating an energetic barrier around yourself, your home, or your sacred space to prevent negative influences from penetrating. Both practices are proactive measures that help maintain your energetic integrity and ensure the success of your magickal work. Protection and shielding are not just for dealing with external threats; they also help manage internal challenges. Negative thoughts, emotions, and stress can create energetic imbalances that affect your practice. By incorporating protection and shielding into your routine, you create a stable foundation for your spiritual growth and magickal endeavors.

Creating a Protective Shield

One of the most effective methods of personal protection is creating an energetic shield around your body. This shield acts as a barrier, filtering out negative energies and allowing only positive influences to reach you. Here's a simple yet powerful technique for creating a protective shield:

1. **Grounding**: Begin by grounding yourself. Sit or stand comfortably, close your eyes, and take a few deep breaths. Visualize roots extending from your feet deep into the earth, anchoring you securely.
2. **Visualization**: Visualize a sphere of bright, white light surrounding your body. See this light forming a protective barrier around you, about an arm's length away from your skin. The light is impenetrable to negative energies but allows positive energies to flow through freely.
3. **Intention**: Set a clear intention for your shield. You might say something like, "I create this shield to protect myself from all negative energies and influences. Only love, light, and positivity may enter."
4. **Reinforcement**: To strengthen your shield, visualize it becoming denser and more radiant. You can also reinforce it with symbols of protection, such as a pentacle, cross, or other sacred symbols.
5. **Maintenance**: Regularly check and reinforce your shield. Visualize it each morning, and refresh it whenever you feel vulnerable or exposed to negative energies.

Protective Rituals for Your Space
Protecting your home or sacred space is crucial for maintaining a safe environment for your magickal work. Here are some effective rituals to safeguard your space:

1. **Salt Barriers**: Salt is a powerful purifier and protector. Sprinkle a line of salt across doorways and windowsills to prevent negative energies from entering. You can also create a salt circle around your home or sacred space for added protection.
2. **Smoke Cleansing**: Use the smoke of sacred herbs like sage, cedar, or palo santo to cleanse and protect your space. Walk through each room, wafting the smoke into corners and dark spaces, while setting the intention to remove all negative energies.
3. **Protective Grids**: Create a protective grid using crystals. Place black tourmaline, clear quartz, and amethyst in the corners of your space. Visualize the crystals forming a protective barrier that repels negativity and enhances the positive energy within.

4. **Wardings and Sigils**: Draw protective sigils or symbols on paper and place them in strategic locations around your home. You can also carve or paint them onto doors, windows, and other entry points. Common symbols include the pentacle, triquetra, and Hamsa hand.
5. **Herbal Sachets**: Create sachets filled with protective herbs such as rosemary, thyme, and bay leaves. Hang these sachets near entrances, in closets, or under your bed to provide ongoing protection.

Protective Amulets and Talismans

Amulets and talismans are powerful tools for personal protection. These objects are charged with specific intentions and energies to guard against harm and attract positive influences. Here's how to create and use protective amulets and talismans:

1. **Choosing Your Object**: Select an object that resonates with you and feels protective. This could be a piece of jewelry, a stone, a small statue, or even a specific item like a key or a coin.

2. **Cleansing**: Cleanse your chosen object to remove any unwanted energies. You can do this by passing it through smoke, placing it in salt, or washing it in water infused with cleansing herbs.
3. **Charging**: Charge the object with your protective intention. Hold it in your hands, visualize it glowing with protective energy, and state your intention clearly. For example, "I charge this amulet to protect me from all harm and negativity."
4. **Blessing**: Perform a blessing ritual to consecrate the object. You can use elements such as earth, air, fire, and water, or call upon deities, spirits, or ancestors to bless the amulet.
5. **Carrying and Using**: Carry the amulet with you, wear it as jewelry, or place it in your home. Regularly recharge and cleanse the amulet to maintain its protective power.

Daily Protective Practices

Incorporating protective practices into your daily routine helps maintain a consistent barrier against negative influences. Here are some simple yet effective daily practices:

1. **Morning Shielding**: Begin each day by visualizing your protective shield. This sets a strong foundation for the day and prepares you to face any challenges.
2. **Affirmations**: Use protective affirmations throughout the day. Examples include, "I am surrounded by a shield of light," or "I am protected and safe." Repeating these affirmations reinforces your protective intent.
3. **Protective Breathing**: Practice protective breathing exercises. Inhale deeply, visualizing positive energy filling your body, and exhale, releasing any negativity. This practice helps to clear and protect your aura.
4. **Herbal Protection**: Carry protective herbs like rosemary, sage, or garlic with you. Place them in a small pouch or wear them in a charm. These herbs provide ongoing protection and support.
5. **Evening Reflection**: At the end of each day, reflect on any negative experiences or energies you encountered. Visualize releasing these energies and reinforcing your protective shield.

Advanced Shielding Techniques
For those who wish to explore more advanced shielding techniques, here are some methods that provide extra layers of protection:

1. **Multi-Layered Shields**: Create multiple layers of protection around yourself. Visualize concentric spheres of light, each with a specific protective quality. For example, the outer layer could repel negative energies, the middle layer could transform negative energies into positive, and the inner layer could provide comfort and strength.
2. **Elemental Shields**: Incorporate the elements into your shielding. Visualize shields made of earth, water, fire, and air, each providing different types of protection. For example, an earth shield could provide grounding and stability, while a fire shield could burn away negativity.
3. **Reflective Shields**: Create a shield that reflects negative energies back to their source. Visualize a mirror-like surface surrounding you, repelling any harmful intentions directed your way. This technique is particularly effective for dealing with psychic attacks or negative people.

4. **Dynamic Shields**: Develop a shield that adapts to different situations. Visualize a flexible, flowing barrier that responds to various energies, strengthening or relaxing as needed. This type of shield provides continuous protection while allowing you to remain open to positive experiences.

Conclusion: Empowering Your Magickal Practice

Protection and shielding are vital components of a robust and effective magickal practice. By incorporating these techniques into your routine, you create a safe and harmonious environment for your spiritual work, ensuring that you remain free from negative influences and fully empowered to manifest your intentions.

Embrace the practices of protection and shielding with dedication and intention. Regularly cleanse, reinforce, and adapt your protective measures to suit your needs and circumstances. As you do so, you will find that your magick flows more smoothly, your energy remains vibrant, and your spiritual growth is supported and safeguarded.

May your journey in protection and shielding bring you strength, security, and a deep sense of peace. With these practices, you are well-equipped to navigate the complexities of the magickal world and thrive in your spiritual endeavors.

Chapter 12: Healing the Body

The Wisdom of Natural Healing

In the intricate dance of life, our bodies are the vessels through which we experience the world. Maintaining their health and vitality is paramount not only for our physical well-being but also for our spiritual and emotional balance. Healing the body through natural magick involves harnessing the power of nature, our innate healing abilities, and ancient wisdom. This chapter delves into the art of using natural magick to heal the body, offering practical techniques and insights to help you restore and maintain optimal health.

The Holistic Approach

Natural healing is grounded in a holistic approach that considers the body, mind, and spirit as interconnected. When one aspect of our being is out of balance, it affects the whole. Healing, therefore, involves addressing the root causes of illness rather than just alleviating symptoms. This perspective aligns with the principles of natural magick, which seeks to harmonize our energies with those of the universe.

A holistic approach to healing includes:

1. **Physical Care**: Proper nutrition, regular exercise, and adequate rest are fundamental. Nourishing the body with wholesome foods, engaging in physical activities, and ensuring sufficient sleep create a strong foundation for health.
2. **Emotional Well-being**: Emotions play a significant role in our health. Practices such as meditation, journaling, and counseling help us process and release emotional stress, fostering emotional balance.
3. **Spiritual Connection**: Spiritual practices, whether through meditation, prayer, or ritual, nourish our spirit and provide a sense of purpose and connection to something greater than ourselves.

Herbal Remedies for Healing

Herbs have been used for centuries to heal the body and support wellness. Each herb carries unique properties that can address specific health concerns. Here are some commonly used herbs and their healing properties:

1. **Echinacea**: Known for its immune-boosting properties, echinacea helps fight off colds and infections. It stimulates the production of white blood cells, enhancing the body's natural defense mechanisms.
2. **Ginger**: A powerful anti-inflammatory and antioxidant, ginger aids digestion, reduces nausea, and alleviates muscle pain. Its warming properties make it ideal for stimulating circulation and relieving congestion.
3. **Turmeric**: Turmeric contains curcumin, a compound with strong anti-inflammatory and antioxidant effects. It supports joint health, reduces inflammation, and promotes overall wellness.
4. **Lavender**: Renowned for its calming effects, lavender helps reduce anxiety, improve sleep, and soothe headaches. It also has antiseptic properties, making it useful for minor cuts and burns.
5. **Peppermint**: Peppermint aids digestion, relieves headaches, and improves respiratory function. Its cooling properties provide relief from muscle tension and pain.

To harness the healing power of herbs, you can create teas, tinctures, and salves. Here's a simple guide to preparing these remedies:

1. **Herbal Tea**: Steep 1-2 teaspoons of dried herbs in a cup of boiling water for 10-15 minutes. Strain and drink. Herbal teas are gentle yet effective, making them ideal for daily use.
2. **Tincture**: Fill a jar with dried herbs and cover them with alcohol (such as vodka) or apple cider vinegar. Seal the jar and let it sit in a dark place for 4-6 weeks, shaking it occasionally. Strain and bottle the tincture. Take in small doses as needed.
3. **Salve**: Infuse herbs in a carrier oil (such as olive or coconut oil) by heating them gently for several hours. Strain the oil and mix it with melted beeswax to create a salve. Apply to the skin for relief from pain, inflammation, or irritation.

Energy Healing Techniques

Energy healing is a vital component of natural magick, focusing on the flow and balance of energy within the body. Various techniques can help clear blockages, restore balance, and promote healing:

1. **Reiki**: Reiki is a Japanese technique that involves channeling universal life energy through the hands to promote healing. Practitioners place their hands on or near the body, allowing the energy to flow and remove blockages.
2. **Chakra Balancing**: The chakras are energy centers within the body that influence our physical, emotional, and spiritual health. Balancing the chakras involves visualizing each chakra, using crystals or essential oils, and meditating to restore their harmonious flow.
3. **Acupressure**: Acupressure involves applying pressure to specific points on the body to relieve pain, reduce stress, and promote healing. These points correspond to energy meridians, and stimulating them helps balance the body's energy flow.

4. **Crystal Healing**: Crystals have unique vibrational frequencies that can influence our energy fields. Placing crystals on or around the body helps clear blockages, restore balance, and enhance overall well-being. Commonly used crystals include amethyst for calming, clear quartz for clarity, and rose quartz for emotional healing.

Mind-Body Techniques

The mind and body are deeply interconnected, and techniques that engage both can have profound healing effects. Here are some practices that harness the power of the mind-body connection:

1. **Meditation**: Meditation calms the mind, reduces stress, and promotes emotional balance. It also enhances self-awareness and helps us connect with our inner wisdom. Regular meditation practice supports overall health and well-being.
2. **Visualization**: Visualization involves imagining the body healing and becoming vibrant and healthy. Visualizing positive outcomes and the body's natural healing processes can stimulate the immune system and accelerate recovery.

3. **Breathwork**: Breathwork practices, such as deep breathing or pranayama, enhance the flow of life force energy (prana) within the body. Controlled breathing techniques reduce stress, increase oxygenation, and promote relaxation and healing.
4. **Yoga**: Yoga combines physical postures, breathwork, and meditation to create a holistic practice that supports physical, emotional, and spiritual health. Regular yoga practice improves flexibility, strength, and mental clarity, promoting overall well-being.

Rituals for Physical Healing

Rituals are powerful tools in natural magick, providing a structured way to focus intention and harness energy for healing. Here are some simple yet effective healing rituals:

1. **Candle Healing Ritual**: Light a green or white candle to represent healing. Sit quietly, focus on the flame, and visualize the healing energy flowing into your body. Speak affirmations such as, "I am healthy, whole, and vibrant." Allow the candle to burn completely, absorbing and releasing any negative energies.
2. **Healing Circle**: Gather a group of like-minded individuals to create a healing circle. Each person takes turns sitting in the center while the others send healing energy, prayers, or positive intentions. This collective energy amplifies the healing process and creates a supportive community.
3. **Herbal Bath Ritual**: Prepare a bath with healing herbs such as lavender, chamomile, or rosemary. Light candles, play soothing music, and soak in the bath, visualizing the water washing away any illness or negative energy. As you soak, repeat affirmations of health and wellness.

4. **Crystal Grid**: Create a crystal grid for healing by arranging crystals in a geometric pattern. Place a clear quartz crystal in the center and surround it with other healing stones. Focus your intention on the grid, visualizing it radiating healing energy throughout your body and space.

Listening to Your Body

One of the most powerful aspects of natural healing is learning to listen to your body's signals. Your body communicates its needs and imbalances through sensations, pain, and intuition. By tuning into these messages, you can address issues before they become serious and support your body's natural healing processes.

1. **Body Scan Meditation**: Practice a body scan meditation to become aware of any areas of tension, discomfort, or imbalance. Start at your toes and slowly move up to your head, noting any sensations without judgment. This practice enhances body awareness and helps you identify areas needing attention.

2. **Intuitive Eating**: Pay attention to your body's signals of hunger and fullness, and choose foods that nourish and support your health. Avoid eating out of habit or emotion, and listen to what your body truly needs.
3. **Rest and Activity Balance**: Balance rest and physical activity to support your body's natural rhythms. Listen to your body's need for rest and recovery, and engage in activities that bring joy and vitality.

Conclusion: Embracing the Path of Natural Healing

Healing the body through natural magick is a journey of self-discovery, empowerment, and connection with the natural world. By integrating herbal remedies, energy healing, mind-body techniques, and rituals into your practice, you create a comprehensive approach to health and well-being.

Remember that healing is not a one-time event but a continuous process of nurturing and balancing your body, mind, and spirit. Stay curious, remain open to new practices, and trust in your body's innate ability to heal.

May your path of natural healing bring you vibrant health, profound wisdom, and a deep sense of harmony and connection with the world around you. Embrace the journey, and let the healing energies of nature guide you toward a life of well-being and fulfillment.

Chapter 13: Calming the Mind

The Sanctuary of a Calm Mind

In the whirlwind of modern life, the mind often becomes a battleground of thoughts, worries, and distractions. Finding tranquility amid the chaos can seem daunting, yet a calm mind is essential for overall well-being and effective magickal practice. A calm mind is a sanctuary where clarity, creativity, and inner peace reside. This chapter explores the art of calming the mind, offering practical techniques and insights to help you cultivate mental stillness and serenity.

The Importance of Mental Calm

Mental calm is the foundation of a balanced and fulfilling life. When the mind is calm, we can think clearly, make better decisions, and respond to challenges with grace and resilience. For magickal practitioners, a calm mind is crucial for focusing intention, visualizing outcomes, and connecting with higher energies. Moreover, mental calmness supports emotional stability, physical health, and spiritual growth.

In contrast, a restless mind can lead to stress, anxiety, and a host of physical ailments. It can cloud our judgment, drain our energy, and hinder our magickal work. Therefore, learning to calm the mind is not just a luxury; it is a vital skill for maintaining harmony in all aspects of life.

Techniques for Calming the Mind

There are numerous techniques for calming the mind, each offering unique benefits. Here are some effective practices to help you cultivate mental tranquility:

1. **Meditation**: Meditation is one of the most powerful tools for calming the mind. It involves focusing your attention and eliminating the stream of jumbled thoughts that may be crowding your mind. Regular meditation practice can reduce stress, enhance self-awareness, and promote emotional health. There are many forms of meditation, such as mindfulness meditation, mantra meditation, and guided meditation. Find a practice that resonates with you and commit to it regularly.

2. **Breathwork**: Conscious breathing techniques can quickly calm the mind and reduce stress. One effective method is deep diaphragmatic breathing, which involves breathing deeply into the belly rather than shallowly into the chest. Another technique is the 4-7-8 breath: inhale for a count of four, hold for seven, and exhale for eight. This pattern helps to activate the body's relaxation response.
3. **Visualization**: Visualization involves using your imagination to create calming and peaceful images in your mind. This can be a powerful way to reduce stress and promote relaxation. Visualize yourself in a serene place, such as a beach, forest, or garden. Engage all your senses in the visualization, imagining the sights, sounds, and smells of the place. This practice can help shift your focus away from stressors and bring a sense of calm.

4. **Mindfulness**: Mindfulness is the practice of being fully present in the moment. It involves observing your thoughts and feelings without judgment. By staying anchored in the present, you can reduce anxiety about the future and regrets about the past. Simple mindfulness exercises include focusing on your breath, paying attention to the sensations in your body, or observing the details of your surroundings.
5. **Journaling**: Writing down your thoughts and feelings can be a therapeutic way to clear your mind. Journaling helps you process emotions, gain clarity, and release mental clutter. Set aside time each day to write freely, without worrying about grammar or structure. Allow your thoughts to flow onto the paper, and you may find that your mind feels lighter and more organized.

Incorporating Nature

Nature has a profound ability to soothe the mind and restore a sense of peace. Spending time in natural settings can help you disconnect from the stressors of daily life and reconnect with the earth's calming energies. Here are some ways to incorporate nature into your practice of calming the mind:

1. **Nature Walks**: Take regular walks in nature, whether it's a park, forest, beach, or garden. Pay attention to the sights, sounds, and smells around you. Walking mindfully in nature can help you feel grounded and present, reducing mental chatter and promoting relaxation.
2. **Grounding**: Grounding, or earthing, involves connecting physically with the earth. Walking barefoot on grass, sand, or soil can help you absorb the earth's stabilizing energies. Grounding can reduce stress, improve mood, and enhance overall well-being.

3. **Gardening**: Gardening is a therapeutic activity that connects you with the cycles of nature. Tending to plants, feeling the soil, and watching things grow can be incredibly calming. Gardening also provides a sense of accomplishment and nurtures a deeper connection with the natural world.
4. **Nature Sounds**: Even if you can't get outside, you can still benefit from the calming effects of nature. Listen to recordings of nature sounds, such as birdsong, flowing water, or rustling leaves. These sounds can create a serene atmosphere and help quiet your mind.

Rituals for Mental Calm

Rituals are structured practices that can bring a sense of order and tranquility to your life. Incorporating rituals for mental calm into your daily routine can help you create a consistent practice of relaxation and mindfulness. Here are some rituals to consider:

1. **Morning Ritual**: Begin your day with a calming ritual that sets a positive tone. This could include meditation, breathwork, or a gratitude practice. Taking a few moments to center yourself in the morning can help you navigate the day with greater ease and focus.
2. **Evening Ritual**: Wind down in the evening with a ritual that helps you release the stresses of the day. This might involve journaling, a warm bath with calming herbs, or a few minutes of mindful breathing. An evening ritual can promote better sleep and ensure you wake up feeling refreshed.
3. **Tea Ceremony**: Create a simple tea ceremony as a daily practice of mindfulness and relaxation. Choose a calming herbal tea, such as chamomile or lavender, and prepare it with intention. As you sip your tea, focus on the warmth, taste, and aroma, allowing yourself to be fully present in the moment.

4. **Candle Meditation**: Light a candle and sit quietly, focusing on the flame. The gentle flickering can be mesmerizing and help to still your mind. As you watch the flame, let go of any intrusive thoughts and immerse yourself in the calming energy of the light.

Herbal Allies for Mental Calm

Herbs can be powerful allies in calming the mind and promoting relaxation. Here are some herbs that are particularly effective for mental calm:

1. **Chamomile**: Chamomile is well-known for its calming effects. Drinking chamomile tea can help reduce anxiety, promote relaxation, and improve sleep.
2. **Lavender**: Lavender has soothing properties that can help alleviate stress and anxiety. Use lavender essential oil in a diffuser, add dried lavender to a bath, or drink lavender tea.
3. **Lemon Balm**: Lemon balm is a gentle yet effective herb for calming the mind and lifting the spirits. It can be taken as a tea or tincture to reduce stress and promote a sense of well-being.

4. **Passionflower**: Passionflower is a natural sedative that can help ease anxiety and promote restful sleep. It can be taken as a tea or tincture before bed.
5. **Ashwagandha**: Ashwagandha is an adaptogenic herb that helps the body cope with stress. It can improve mood, reduce anxiety, and promote mental clarity. It is often taken as a supplement or in powdered form.

Conclusion: Embracing Mental Calm
Cultivating a calm mind is a journey of self-discovery and practice. By integrating techniques such as meditation, breathwork, visualization, and rituals into your daily routine, you can create a sanctuary of mental calm amidst the chaos of modern life. Remember that mental calmness is not about eliminating all thoughts but about finding a sense of peace and clarity within the mind's natural ebb and flow.

Embrace the practices that resonate with you and make them a regular part of your life. With patience and consistency, you will find that a calm mind becomes a natural state of being, enhancing your overall well-being and magickal practice.

May your journey towards mental calm be filled with moments of tranquility, insight, and profound peace. Let the wisdom of natural magick guide you to a place of inner serenity and mental clarity, where you can fully realize your potential and embrace the beauty of each moment.

Chapter 14: Emotional Balance

The Essence of Emotional Balance

In the quest for well-being and personal growth, achieving emotional balance is fundamental. Emotions are the threads that weave through the fabric of our lives, influencing our thoughts, actions, and interactions. When emotions are balanced, they enrich our experiences and provide a foundation for mental clarity, physical health, and spiritual growth. However, when emotions are out of balance, they can lead to stress, anxiety, and physical ailments. This chapter explores the art of cultivating emotional balance, offering practical techniques and insights to help you navigate the complexities of your emotional landscape.

Understanding Emotional Balance

Emotional balance does not mean suppressing or avoiding emotions; rather, it involves recognizing, understanding, and managing them in a healthy way. It is about experiencing the full spectrum of emotions without being overwhelmed by them. Achieving emotional balance allows you to respond to life's challenges with resilience and grace, maintaining a sense of inner peace and stability.

Emotional balance involves:

1. **Awareness**: Being aware of your emotions as they arise and understanding their impact on your thoughts and actions.
2. **Acceptance**: Accepting your emotions without judgment, recognizing that all emotions, whether positive or negative, are valid and serve a purpose.
3. **Regulation**: Developing healthy strategies to manage and express emotions, preventing them from becoming overwhelming or destructive.

Techniques for Cultivating Emotional Balance

There are numerous techniques that can help you achieve and maintain emotional balance. Here are some effective practices:

1. **Mindfulness Meditation**: Mindfulness meditation involves observing your thoughts and emotions without judgment. By staying present and fully experiencing your emotions, you can gain insights into their origins and patterns. Regular mindfulness practice helps to reduce emotional reactivity and increase emotional awareness.

2. **Journaling**: Writing down your thoughts and emotions can be a powerful tool for emotional processing. Journaling provides a safe space to explore your feelings, identify patterns, and gain clarity. Set aside time each day to write freely about your experiences and emotions.
3. **Breathwork**: Breathwork techniques, such as deep diaphragmatic breathing or alternate nostril breathing, can help regulate your emotional state. Controlled breathing activates the body's relaxation response, reducing stress and promoting emotional calm.
4. **Emotional Freedom Techniques (EFT)**: Also known as tapping, EFT involves tapping on specific meridian points on the body while focusing on a particular emotion or issue. This practice helps to release emotional blockages and restore balance.

5. **Visualization**: Visualization involves creating mental images that evoke feelings of peace and balance. Visualize yourself in a calm, safe place, or imagine a protective shield around you that filters out negative emotions. Visualization can help shift your emotional state and provide a sense of control.

Connecting with Nature

Nature has a profound ability to restore emotional balance. Spending time in natural settings can help you disconnect from stressors and reconnect with your inner self. Here are some ways to incorporate nature into your practice:

1. **Nature Walks**: Take regular walks in nature, paying attention to the sights, sounds, and smells around you. Walking mindfully in nature can help ground you and provide a sense of peace.
2. **Gardening**: Gardening is a therapeutic activity that connects you with the cycles of nature. Tending to plants, feeling the soil, and watching things grow can be incredibly calming and emotionally fulfilling.

3. **Grounding**: Grounding, or earthing, involves connecting physically with the earth. Walking barefoot on grass, sand, or soil can help you absorb the earth's stabilizing energies, reducing emotional stress and promoting balance.
4. **Nature Sounds**: Even if you can't get outside, you can benefit from the calming effects of nature. Listen to recordings of nature sounds, such as birdsong, flowing water, or rustling leaves, to create a serene atmosphere and help balance your emotions.

Rituals for Emotional Balance

Rituals provide structure and intention to your efforts to achieve emotional balance. Incorporating rituals into your daily routine can help create a sense of order and stability. Here are some rituals to consider:

1. **Morning Grounding Ritual**: Begin your day with a grounding ritual to center yourself and set a positive tone. Sit quietly, take a few deep breaths, and visualize roots extending from your feet into the earth. Feel the stability and support of the earth, and set an intention for the day.

2. **Evening Reflection Ritual**: End your day with a reflection ritual to release any accumulated stress and emotions. Light a candle, sit quietly, and reflect on your day. Acknowledge any challenging emotions, and visualize them being released into the flame. Express gratitude for the positive moments.
3. **Herbal Bath Ritual**: Prepare a soothing herbal bath with calming herbs such as lavender, chamomile, or rose petals. As you soak in the bath, visualize the water washing away any negative emotions and restoring balance. Use this time for relaxation and self-care.
4. **Candle Meditation**: Light a candle and sit quietly, focusing on the flame. The gentle flickering can be mesmerizing and help to still your mind. As you watch the flame, let go of any intrusive thoughts and immerse yourself in the calming energy of the light.

Herbal Allies for Emotional Balance

Herbs can be powerful allies in achieving emotional balance. Here are some herbs that are particularly effective:

1. **Chamomile**: Chamomile is well-known for its calming effects. Drinking chamomile tea can help reduce anxiety and promote relaxation.
2. **Lavender**: Lavender has soothing properties that can help alleviate stress and anxiety. Use lavender essential oil in a diffuser, add dried lavender to a bath, or drink lavender tea.
3. **Lemon Balm**: Lemon balm is a gentle yet effective herb for lifting the spirits and promoting emotional balance. It can be taken as a tea or tincture.
4. **Passionflower**: Passionflower is a natural sedative that can help ease anxiety and promote restful sleep. It can be taken as a tea or tincture before bed.
5. **Rose**: Rose is associated with love and emotional healing. Rose petals can be used in teas, baths, or as an essential oil to soothe the heart and promote feelings of peace and well-being.

Emotional Release Techniques

Sometimes, achieving emotional balance requires releasing pent-up emotions. Here are some techniques for emotional release:

1. **Creative Expression**: Engaging in creative activities such as painting, drawing, or writing can help release emotions. Allow yourself to express your feelings freely through your chosen medium.
2. **Physical Activity**: Exercise can be a powerful way to release emotional tension. Activities such as running, dancing, or yoga help to move energy through the body and release stress.
3. **Crying**: Allowing yourself to cry can be a healthy way to release emotions. Crying is a natural process that helps to cleanse the body of stress hormones and restore balance.
4. **Sound Healing**: Using sound to release emotions can be very effective. Singing, chanting, or playing a musical instrument can help to move and release emotional energy.

Seeking Support

Achieving emotional balance can sometimes be challenging, and it's important to seek support when needed. Here are some ways to find support:

1. **Therapy**: Speaking with a therapist can provide valuable insights and tools for managing emotions. Therapy offers a safe space to explore your feelings and develop healthy coping strategies.
2. **Support Groups**: Joining a support group can provide a sense of community and connection. Sharing your experiences with others who understand can be incredibly validating and healing.
3. **Friends and Family**: Lean on your friends and family for support. Talking to someone you trust can help you gain perspective and feel less alone in your struggles.
4. **Spiritual Guidance**: Seek guidance from a spiritual advisor or mentor. Spiritual practices and insights can provide comfort and help you find meaning in your experiences.

Conclusion: Embracing Emotional Balance

Cultivating emotional balance is a journey of self-discovery and growth. By integrating techniques such as mindfulness meditation, journaling, breathwork, and rituals into your daily routine, you can achieve a sense of emotional stability and peace. Remember that emotional balance is not about eliminating all negative emotions but about learning to navigate them with grace and resilience.

Embrace the practices that resonate with you and make them a regular part of your life. With patience and consistency, you will find that emotional balance becomes a natural state of being, enhancing your overall well-being and enriching your magickal practice.

May your journey toward emotional balance be filled with moments of insight, healing, and profound peace. Let the wisdom of natural magick guide you to a place of inner harmony and emotional clarity, where you can fully embrace the beauty and complexity of your emotional landscape.

Chapter 15: Dream Magick and Sleep

The Mystical Realm of Dreams

Dreams are a gateway to a world where the boundaries of reality blur and the subconscious mind reveals its secrets. For centuries, dreams have been a source of inspiration, guidance, and prophecy. They offer insights into our deepest fears, desires, and the unseen forces that shape our lives. Dream magick harnesses the power of this mystical realm, transforming sleep into a time for spiritual exploration and magickal work. In this chapter, we will explore the art of dream magick and the practices that can enhance your sleep, leading to deeper, more meaningful dreams.

The Power of Dreams

Dreams have fascinated humanity for millennia. In ancient cultures, dreams were often regarded as messages from the gods or the spirit world. Shamans, mystics, and seers used dreams to gain insight, solve problems, and predict the future. Today, we understand that dreams are a natural part of the sleep cycle, serving various psychological and physiological functions. However, their magickal potential remains as potent as ever.

Dream magick involves using the dream state for magickal purposes, such as receiving guidance, healing, and connecting with higher realms. It is a form of active dreaming where the dreamer sets intentions and employs techniques to influence and interact with their dreams. By integrating dream magick into your practice, you can unlock the transformative power of your dreams and enhance your spiritual journey.

Enhancing Sleep for Dream Work

Quality sleep is essential for effective dream work. The following practices can help you create an optimal environment for restful sleep and vivid dreaming:

1. **Create a Sacred Sleep Space**: Your bedroom should be a sanctuary for rest and relaxation. Keep it clean, clutter-free, and free of electronic distractions. Incorporate calming colors, soft lighting, and natural elements to create a peaceful atmosphere. Consider placing crystals such as amethyst or moonstone near your bed to enhance dream work.
2. **Establish a Sleep Routine**: Consistency is key to promoting healthy sleep patterns. Establish a regular sleep schedule by going to bed and waking up at the same time each day. Create a bedtime ritual that signals to your body and mind that it's time to wind down. This could include activities such as reading, taking a warm bath, or practicing gentle stretches.
3. **Limit Stimulants**: Avoid consuming caffeine, nicotine, and alcohol close to bedtime, as these substances can interfere with sleep quality. Instead, opt for calming herbal teas such as chamomile, valerian root, or lavender to promote relaxation.

4. **Disconnect from Electronics**: The blue light emitted by screens can disrupt your body's natural sleep-wake cycle. Turn off electronic devices at least an hour before bed and engage in calming activities that don't involve screens.
5. **Use Aromatherapy**: Essential oils such as lavender, sandalwood, and bergamot have calming properties that can enhance sleep. Use a diffuser, apply diluted oils to your pulse points, or sprinkle a few drops on your pillow to create a soothing environment.

Preparing for Dream Magick

To effectively engage in dream magick, it's important to prepare both mentally and physically. Here are some steps to set the stage for successful dream work:

1. **Set Intentions**: Before going to bed, set clear intentions for your dream work. What do you hope to achieve or discover in your dreams? Whether it's receiving guidance, solving a problem, or connecting with a specific entity, clearly stating your intention helps focus your subconscious mind.

2. **Keep a Dream Journal**: Place a journal and pen beside your bed to record your dreams immediately upon waking. This practice helps you remember your dreams more clearly and track patterns or recurring symbols. Writing down your dreams also reinforces the importance of dream work in your mind.
3. **Create a Dream Talisman**: A dream talisman is an object imbued with the intention to enhance your dream work. This could be a crystal, a piece of jewelry, or a small charm. Hold the talisman in your hands, visualize your intention, and ask for its assistance in your dream work. Place it under your pillow or beside your bed while you sleep.
4. **Practice Dream Affirmations**: Recite affirmations before bed to program your subconscious mind for successful dream work. Examples include, "I remember my dreams clearly," "My dreams provide guidance and insight," or "I am open to receiving messages in my dreams."

Techniques for Dream Magick

There are various techniques you can use to influence and enhance your dreams for magickal purposes. Here are some effective methods:

1. **Lucid Dreaming**: Lucid dreaming is the practice of becoming aware that you are dreaming while still in the dream state. This awareness allows you to consciously interact with your dream environment. To induce lucid dreams, practice reality checks during the day (such as looking at your hands and asking if you are dreaming), keep a dream journal, and set the intention to become lucid before bed. Once lucid, you can explore your dreams, seek guidance, and perform magickal work.
2. **Dream Incubation**: Dream incubation involves planting a specific idea or question in your mind before sleep with the intention of receiving an answer in your dreams. Write down your question or intention, meditate on it, and visualize receiving an answer. Place the written intention under your pillow and repeat it to yourself as you fall asleep.

3. **Dream Altar**: Create a small altar dedicated to dream work. Include items that represent your intentions, such as crystals, candles, herbs, and symbols. Light a candle and focus on your intention before bed, asking for guidance and clarity in your dreams. This ritual helps to strengthen your connection to the dream realm.
4. **Astral Travel**: Astral travel, or astral projection, involves consciously leaving your physical body and exploring the astral plane. This can be achieved through deep meditation and visualization techniques. Before sleep, relax your body and visualize yourself floating above your physical form. Set the intention to explore the astral plane in your dreams and seek knowledge or guidance.

Interpreting Your Dreams

Interpreting your dreams is a crucial part of dream magick. Dreams often communicate through symbols and metaphors, and understanding their meaning can provide valuable insights. Here are some tips for interpreting your dreams:

1. **Look for Patterns**: Review your dream journal regularly and look for recurring themes, symbols, or emotions. These patterns can reveal important messages from your subconscious mind.
2. **Personal Associations**: Consider what the symbols in your dreams mean to you personally. While there are common interpretations for many symbols, your unique experiences and associations can provide deeper insights.
3. **Emotional Tone**: Pay attention to the emotions you experience in your dreams. The emotional tone can offer clues about the underlying message. For example, a feeling of fear might indicate an unresolved issue or hidden fear, while a sense of peace could signify acceptance or resolution.
4. **Seek Guidance**: If you're having trouble interpreting a dream, consider seeking guidance from a trusted friend, mentor, or spiritual advisor. Sometimes, an outside perspective can provide clarity and new insights.

Using Dreams for Healing

Dreams can be a powerful tool for healing, both physically and emotionally. Here are some ways to use dreams for healing purposes:

1. **Healing Dreams**: Set the intention to receive healing in your dreams. Before bed, visualize healing energy surrounding your body and ask for guidance on how to heal a specific issue. Pay attention to any dreams that offer insights or solutions related to your health.
2. **Emotional Release**: Dreams can help you process and release unresolved emotions. If you experience a particularly emotional dream, reflect on its meaning and allow yourself to feel and release the emotions. This can lead to emotional healing and resolution.
3. **Nightmares**: Nightmares can be distressing, but they often carry important messages. Instead of avoiding or fearing them, approach nightmares with curiosity. Reflect on what they might be revealing about your fears or unresolved issues, and use the insights to promote healing and growth.

4. **Dream Rehearsal**: If you have recurring nightmares or troubling dreams, try dream rehearsal. Visualize a positive outcome for the dream before bed and imagine yourself responding to the situation with confidence and calm. This technique can help reprogram your subconscious mind and reduce the occurrence of negative dreams.

Conclusion: Embracing Dream Magick

Dream magick is a powerful and transformative practice that allows you to explore the depths of your subconscious mind and connect with higher realms. By enhancing your sleep, preparing for dream work, and using specific techniques, you can unlock the magickal potential of your dreams and enrich your spiritual journey. Embrace the practices that resonate with you and make dream magick a regular part of your life. With dedication and intention, you will find that your dreams become a source of guidance, healing, and inspiration.

May your journey into the realm of dreams be filled with wonder, insight, and magick. Let the mysteries of the dream world guide you toward greater understanding and spiritual growth, and may your dreams always be a source of wisdom and illumination.

Chapter 16: Meditative Practices

The Art of Stillness

In the cacophony of modern life, finding moments of stillness can be profoundly transformative. Meditation, the practice of focused attention and mindfulness, offers a sanctuary for the mind and spirit. It is a timeless art that brings clarity, peace, and a deep connection to the inner self. In this chapter, we will explore various meditative practices, guiding you through techniques that can enhance your spiritual journey and bring balance to your life.

The Power of Meditation

Meditation is a powerful tool for personal growth and spiritual development. It helps to quiet the mind, reduce stress, and foster a sense of inner peace. By regularly engaging in meditation, you can cultivate a heightened awareness of your thoughts, emotions, and surroundings. This practice not only improves mental and emotional well-being but also enhances your magickal work by sharpening your focus and intention.

Meditation has been practiced for thousands of years across various cultures and spiritual traditions. From the mindfulness meditation of Buddhism to the contemplative prayer of Christianity, meditation is a universal practice that transcends boundaries. Its benefits are well-documented, including improved concentration, emotional stability, and even physical health.

Preparing for Meditation

Creating the right environment and mindset for meditation is essential for a successful practice. Here are some steps to prepare for your meditation sessions:

1. **Choose a Quiet Space**: Select a quiet, comfortable space where you can meditate without interruptions. This could be a dedicated meditation room, a corner of your home, or a peaceful outdoor spot. Ensure the space is clean, clutter-free, and inviting.
2. **Set the Mood**: Create a calming atmosphere with soft lighting, soothing music, or nature sounds. You might also light a candle or burn incense to enhance the ambiance. Aromatherapy with essential oils like lavender, sandalwood, or frankincense can also help you relax.

3. **Comfortable Posture**: Sit in a comfortable position with your spine straight. You can sit on a chair, cushion, or the floor. Ensure that your body is relaxed and supported. If sitting is uncomfortable, you can lie down, but be mindful not to fall asleep.
4. **Mindset and Intention**: Approach your meditation practice with an open mind and a clear intention. Whether you aim to reduce stress, gain clarity, or deepen your spiritual connection, setting an intention helps focus your practice.

Basic Meditation Techniques

There are many meditation techniques, each with its own unique approach and benefits. Here are some foundational practices to get you started:

1. **Mindfulness Meditation**: Mindfulness meditation involves paying attention to the present moment without judgment. Focus on your breath, noticing the sensation of each inhale and exhale. When your mind wanders, gently bring your attention back to your breath. This practice helps cultivate awareness and acceptance.

2. **Guided Meditation**: In guided meditation, a narrator leads you through a series of visualizations and instructions. This can be particularly helpful for beginners or those seeking specific outcomes like relaxation, healing, or spiritual connection. You can find guided meditations online, on apps, or through meditation teachers.
3. **Mantra Meditation**: Mantra meditation involves repeating a word or phrase, either silently or aloud, to focus the mind. Common mantras include "Om," "Peace," or personal affirmations. The repetition helps to anchor your mind and create a sense of inner calm.
4. **Body Scan Meditation**: This practice involves systematically focusing on different parts of your body, from head to toe, and observing any sensations. The body scan helps to release tension and cultivate a deeper awareness of your physical state.

5. **Loving-Kindness Meditation**: Also known as Metta meditation, this practice involves sending loving-kindness to yourself and others. Begin by focusing on yourself and silently repeating phrases like "May I be happy, may I be healthy, may I be at peace." Gradually extend these wishes to loved ones, acquaintances, and even those with whom you have conflicts.

Advanced Meditation Practices

Once you have established a basic meditation practice, you may wish to explore more advanced techniques. These practices can deepen your meditation experience and enhance your spiritual growth:

1. **Chakra Meditation**: Chakra meditation focuses on the seven energy centers within the body. Visualize each chakra as a spinning wheel of light, starting at the base of the spine and moving up to the crown of the head. Focus on balancing and clearing each chakra, using corresponding colors and affirmations.

2. **Transcendental Meditation (TM)**: TM is a specific form of mantra meditation that involves silently repeating a unique mantra assigned by a certified teacher. The practice aims to transcend ordinary thought and reach a state of deep, restful awareness. TM is typically practiced for 20 minutes twice a day.
3. **Zen Meditation (Zazen)**: Zazen is the practice of seated meditation in the Zen Buddhist tradition. Sit with a straight spine, hands resting in the lap, and eyes half-closed. Focus on your breath and maintain a state of open awareness, allowing thoughts to come and go without attachment.
4. **Visualization Meditation**: This practice involves creating vivid mental images to achieve specific outcomes. Visualize a peaceful scene, a protective shield, or a successful goal. Engaging all your senses in the visualization makes it more powerful and effective.

5. **Walking Meditation**: Walking meditation combines movement with mindfulness. Walk slowly and deliberately, paying attention to each step and the sensations in your body. This practice helps to ground you in the present moment and can be especially beneficial for those who find sitting meditation challenging.

Integrating Meditation into Daily Life
To reap the full benefits of meditation, it's important to integrate it into your daily routine. Here are some tips for making meditation a regular part of your life:

1. **Start Small**: Begin with just a few minutes of meditation each day and gradually increase the duration as you become more comfortable. Consistency is more important than length, so aim for regular practice even if it's brief.
2. **Schedule It**: Set aside a specific time each day for meditation. Treat it as a non-negotiable appointment with yourself. Early morning or before bed are often ideal times for meditation, but find what works best for you.

3. **Create Rituals**: Establish rituals around your meditation practice to make it special and meaningful. Light a candle, say a prayer, or ring a bell to signal the start and end of your session. Rituals help to anchor your practice and create a sense of sacredness.
4. **Mindful Moments**: Incorporate mindfulness into your daily activities. Practice being fully present during routine tasks like eating, walking, or washing dishes. These mindful moments can enhance your overall sense of awareness and presence.
5. **Join a Community**: Meditation can be a solitary practice, but joining a group or community can provide support and encouragement. Look for local meditation groups, classes, or online communities where you can share experiences and learn from others.

Overcoming Challenges

Meditation is a simple practice, but it's not always easy. You may encounter challenges such as restlessness, boredom, or difficulty quieting your mind. Here are some tips for overcoming common obstacles:

1. **Restlessness**: If you feel restless or fidgety during meditation, try a more active form like walking meditation or yoga. Incorporating movement can help release excess energy and make stillness more accessible.
2. **Boredom**: Boredom is a natural part of the meditation process. Instead of resisting it, observe it with curiosity. Notice how boredom feels in your body and mind, and gently bring your focus back to your practice.
3. **Busy Mind**: A busy mind is normal, especially in the beginning. Instead of trying to force your mind to be quiet, simply observe your thoughts without judgment. Allow them to come and go, and gently return your focus to your breath or mantra.
4. **Inconsistency**: If you struggle with maintaining a regular practice, try setting smaller, achievable goals. Use reminders or alarms to prompt you, and reward yourself for your consistency. Remember that meditation is a practice, and it's okay to have ups and downs.

The Benefits of Meditation

The benefits of meditation are profound and far-reaching. Regular practice can lead to:

1. **Reduced Stress**: Meditation activates the body's relaxation response, reducing stress hormones and promoting a sense of calm.
2. **Improved Focus**: Meditation enhances concentration and attention, helping you stay focused and productive.
3. **Emotional Stability**: Meditation helps regulate emotions, making it easier to manage stress, anxiety, and depression.
4. **Enhanced Creativity**: A calm and focused mind can lead to greater creativity and problem-solving abilities.
5. **Spiritual Growth**: Meditation deepens your connection to your inner self and the universe, fostering spiritual insights and growth.

Conclusion: Embracing Meditation

Meditation is a journey of self-discovery and transformation. By incorporating meditative practices into your daily life, you can cultivate inner peace, clarity, and spiritual connection. Whether you are a beginner or an experienced practitioner, there is always more to explore and discover on the path of meditation.

Embrace the practices that resonate with you and make them a regular part of your life. With patience and consistency, you will find that meditation becomes a source of strength, insight, and joy.

May your journey in meditation be filled with moments of stillness, awareness, and profound peace. Let the art of meditation guide you to a place of inner harmony and spiritual enlightenment, where you can fully realize your potential and embrace the beauty of each moment.

Chapter 17: Astral and Spiritual Healing

Beyond the Physical: The Realms of Astral and Spiritual Healing

Our existence transcends the physical body, extending into the astral and spiritual realms. While physical health is essential, addressing imbalances on the astral and spiritual levels can lead to profound healing and transformation. Astral and spiritual healing involve working with the subtle energies and higher aspects of our being to restore harmony and promote well-being. This chapter explores the fascinating world of astral and spiritual healing, offering techniques and insights to help you harness these powerful modalities for personal growth and holistic wellness.

Understanding Astral and Spiritual Healing

Astral healing focuses on the subtle body, often referred to as the astral body, which exists alongside our physical form. This body is composed of energy and is the vehicle through which we experience dreams, emotions, and out-of-body experiences. Spiritual healing, on the other hand, deals with the higher aspects of our existence, such as the soul and spirit, addressing the deeper layers of our being that connect us to the divine.

Healing on these levels involves clearing blockages, restoring balance, and enhancing the flow of energy. It can lead to profound shifts in consciousness, emotional release, and physical healing. By integrating astral and spiritual healing into your practice, you can achieve a more holistic approach to health and well-being.

Techniques for Astral Healing

Astral healing techniques focus on the subtle body and the energy field surrounding it. These practices help to clear negative energies, repair energetic damage, and enhance the overall flow of energy. Here are some effective techniques for astral healing:

1. **Aura Cleansing**: The aura is the energy field that surrounds the physical body, reflecting our physical, emotional, and spiritual state. Cleansing the aura helps to remove negative energies and restore balance. You can cleanse your aura using various methods, such as:
   - **Smoke Cleansing**: Pass the smoke of sage, cedar, or palo santo around your body, visualizing the smoke carrying away any negative energies.
   - **Visualization**: Imagine a bright, golden light surrounding your body, dissolving any dark or heavy energy in your aura.
   - **Crystals**: Use crystals like selenite or clear quartz to sweep through your aura, removing blockages and restoring clarity.

2. **Chakra Healing**: Chakras are energy centers within the body that regulate the flow of energy. Blocked or imbalanced chakras can lead to physical and emotional issues. Healing the chakras involves clearing blockages and restoring balance. Here's how to work with your chakras:
   - **Meditation**: Sit quietly and visualize each chakra as a spinning wheel of light. Start at the base of the spine and move up to the crown of the head, focusing on clearing and balancing each chakra.
   - **Sound Healing**: Use sound frequencies to balance the chakras. Chanting the seed sounds (Bija mantras) for each chakra or listening to chakra tuning frequencies can be very effective.
   - **Crystals and Oils**: Place crystals like amethyst, citrine, and rose quartz on the corresponding chakras, or use essential oils like frankincense, lavender, and sandalwood to enhance healing.

3. **Astral Projection**: Astral projection, or out-of-body experiences, involves consciously leaving the physical body to explore the astral plane. This practice can provide deep insights and healing. Here's how to prepare for astral projection:
   - **Relaxation and Meditation**: Begin with deep relaxation and meditation to calm the mind and body. Use techniques like progressive muscle relaxation or guided meditation to achieve a deeply relaxed state.
   - **Visualization**: Visualize yourself floating above your physical body. Focus on the sensations of lightness and freedom as you imagine yourself exploring the astral plane.
   - **Intentions and Protection**: Set clear intentions for your astral journey and ask for protection from your spirit guides or higher self. This ensures a safe and purposeful experience.

Techniques for Spiritual Healing

Spiritual healing addresses the deeper aspects of our being, connecting us with our higher self, spirit guides, and the divine. These practices promote spiritual growth, emotional healing, and a deeper sense of purpose. Here are some powerful techniques for spiritual healing:

1. **Prayer and Invocation**: Prayer is a powerful tool for connecting with the divine and seeking guidance and healing. Whether you follow a specific religious tradition or have a personal spiritual practice, prayer can be a source of comfort and strength. Here's how to incorporate prayer into your healing practice:
    - **Daily Prayer**: Set aside time each day for prayer. Express gratitude, seek guidance, and ask for healing and protection. Use words that resonate with you, whether they are traditional prayers or personal affirmations.
    - **Invocations**: Call upon your spirit guides, angels, or higher self for assistance. Speak or think your invocation, asking for their presence and support in your healing journey.

2. **Reiki and Energy Healing**: Reiki is a form of energy healing that involves channeling universal life force energy through the hands to promote healing and balance. It can be practiced on yourself or others. Here's a basic self-Reiki practice:
    - **Grounding and Centering**: Begin by grounding yourself and setting a clear intention for healing. Take a few deep breaths and visualize roots extending from your feet into the earth.
    - **Hand Positions**: Place your hands on or just above your body in various positions, starting at the crown of the head and moving down to the feet. Hold each position for a few minutes, allowing the energy to flow and balance.
    - **Closing**: End the session by expressing gratitude and grounding yourself again. Visualize the healing energy integrating into your body and aura.

3. **Spirit Journeying**: Spirit journeying involves traveling to other realms or dimensions to seek guidance, healing, and wisdom from spirit allies and guides. This practice can be facilitated through drumming, chanting, or guided visualization. Here's a basic framework for spirit journeying:
    - **Preparation**: Create a sacred space and set your intention for the journey. Use tools like drums, rattles, or shamanic music to facilitate an altered state of consciousness.
    - **Journeying**: Close your eyes and visualize yourself entering a gateway or portal to another realm. Follow your intuition and allow yourself to be guided by your spirit allies. Ask questions, seek healing, and receive guidance.
    - **Integration**: After the journey, take time to reflect on your experiences and insights. Write them down in a journal and consider how you can integrate them into your daily life.

Integrating Astral and Spiritual Healing into Daily Life

To fully benefit from astral and spiritual healing, it's important to integrate these practices into your daily life. Here are some tips for making these practices a regular part of your routine:

1. **Daily Meditation and Reflection**: Set aside time each day for meditation and reflection. Use this time to connect with your higher self, seek guidance, and clear any energetic blockages.
2. **Regular Energy Cleansing**: Incorporate regular energy cleansing practices into your routine. Use techniques like aura cleansing, chakra balancing, and grounding to maintain energetic balance and clarity.
3. **Spiritual Practices**: Engage in regular spiritual practices that resonate with you, such as prayer, yoga, or mindfulness. These practices help to deepen your connection with the divine and promote overall well-being.

4. **Journaling**: Keep a journal to record your experiences, insights, and progress in astral and spiritual healing. Writing helps to clarify your thoughts and emotions and provides a valuable record of your spiritual journey.
5. **Seek Guidance**: Don't hesitate to seek guidance from spiritual mentors, healers, or teachers. Their wisdom and support can be invaluable in your healing journey.

Conclusion: Embracing the Path of Healing

Astral and spiritual healing offer profound opportunities for growth, transformation, and holistic well-being. By integrating these practices into your life, you can achieve a deeper connection with your higher self, clear energetic blockages, and promote healing on all levels of your being.

Embrace the practices that resonate with you and make them a regular part of your spiritual journey. With dedication and intention, you will find that astral and spiritual healing become powerful tools for personal and spiritual growth.

May your journey in astral and spiritual healing be filled with moments of insight, transformation, and profound peace. Let the wisdom of the subtle realms guide you toward greater understanding, healing, and spiritual enlightenment, where you can fully embrace your true potential and the beauty of your spiritual path.

Chapter 18: Seasonal Rituals

Embracing the Cycles of Nature

The natural world moves in cycles, marked by the changing seasons that bring shifts in light, temperature, and energy. These cycles, from the budding growth of spring to the quiet introspection of winter, reflect the rhythms of life itself. Seasonal rituals are a way to connect with these natural rhythms, align our lives with the cycles of the earth, and draw upon the unique energies each season offers. This chapter explores the power of seasonal rituals, guiding you through practices that honor the turning of the wheel of the year and help you cultivate harmony and balance.

The Importance of Seasonal Rituals

Seasonal rituals are a way to mark the passage of time and celebrate the cyclical nature of life. They provide opportunities to reflect, set intentions, and honor the changing energies of the natural world. Engaging in these rituals helps us stay connected to the earth and its rhythms, fostering a sense of belonging and continuity.

Each season brings its own themes and energies, which can be harnessed for personal growth, healing, and magickal work. By aligning our actions and intentions with the seasons, we can enhance our well-being and create a deeper sense of harmony with the world around us.

Celebrating the Seasons
Here, we explore rituals for each of the four main seasons, offering ways to honor their unique energies and themes.

Spring: Renewal and Rebirth
Spring is a time of renewal, rebirth, and growth. The days grow longer, the earth warms, and new life begins to emerge. This season is ideal for setting new intentions, planting seeds (both literal and metaphorical), and embracing new beginnings.

1. **Spring Equinox Ritual**: The Spring Equinox, also known as Ostara, marks the balance of day and night. It's a time to celebrate balance, renewal, and the return of light. Create an altar with symbols of spring, such as flowers, eggs, and green candles. Meditate on your goals and intentions for the coming months, and plant seeds as a symbol of your new beginnings. As you plant each seed, visualize your intentions taking root and growing.
2. **Nature Walk and Reflection**: Take a mindful walk in nature, observing the signs of spring around you. Notice the budding trees, blooming flowers, and the songs of birds. Reflect on areas of your life where you wish to experience growth and renewal. Collect natural items, such as flowers and stones, to create a spring altar at home.

3. **Spring Cleaning and Purification**: Spring is an ideal time for physical and energetic cleansing. Clear out clutter, clean your home, and create space for new energy to flow. Perform a purification ritual by smudging your space with sage or using a saltwater spray. As you clean, set the intention to release old, stagnant energy and welcome fresh, vibrant energy.

Summer: Abundance and Vitality

Summer is a season of abundance, vitality, and celebration. The days are long and warm, and the earth is in full bloom. This is a time to celebrate achievements, enjoy the fruits of your labor, and connect with the vibrant energy of life.

1. **Summer Solstice Ritual**: The Summer Solstice, also known as Litha or Midsummer, is the longest day of the year. It's a time to celebrate the peak of light and life's abundance. Create an outdoor altar with sun symbols, bright flowers, and candles. Light a bonfire or candles to honor the sun's energy. Reflect on your achievements and express gratitude for the abundance in your life. Perform a dance or make music to celebrate the joy and vitality of summer.
2. **Harvest and Gratitude**: As summer progresses, focus on the theme of harvest and gratitude. Collect herbs, fruits, and vegetables from your garden or local market. Prepare a meal using these fresh ingredients and share it with loved ones. As you eat, give thanks for the abundance of the earth and the efforts that have brought you to this point.

3. **Sun Meditation**: Spend time meditating in the sun, absorbing its warmth and energy. Visualize the sun's rays filling you with vitality and strength. Focus on areas of your life where you want to experience growth and success. Allow the sun's energy to recharge and invigorate you.

Autumn: Reflection and Release

Autumn is a time of reflection, release, and preparation for the coming winter. The days grow shorter, the air cools, and the leaves change color and fall. This season is ideal for letting go of what no longer serves you and harvesting the lessons of the past year.

1. **Autumn Equinox Ritual**: The Autumn Equinox, also known as Mabon, marks the balance of day and night and the beginning of the harvest season. Create an altar with autumn leaves, pumpkins, and candles in warm colors. Reflect on the past year and the goals you set in spring. Celebrate your achievements and acknowledge the lessons learned. Write down what you wish to release and let go of, and burn the paper as a symbol of release.

2. **Gratitude Practice**: Autumn is a time for gratitude and thanksgiving. Create a daily or weekly gratitude practice, where you write down things you are grateful for. This practice helps to cultivate a positive mindset and appreciate the abundance in your life, even as the days grow shorter.
3. **Cleansing and Release**: Perform a ritual to release what no longer serves you. This could be a physical, emotional, or energetic release. Write down what you wish to let go of, and bury the paper in the earth or burn it in a fire. As you perform this ritual, visualize the energy being transformed and released.

Winter: Introspection and Renewal
Winter is a season of introspection, rest, and renewal. The days are short and dark, encouraging us to turn inward and reflect. This is a time for inner work, setting intentions for the new year, and nurturing your inner light.

1. **Winter Solstice Ritual**: The Winter Solstice, also known as Yule, marks the longest night of the year and the return of the light. Create an altar with evergreen branches, candles, and symbols of light. Light a candle to represent the returning sun and meditate on your hopes and intentions for the new year. Reflect on the past year and release any lingering negativity. Celebrate the promise of new beginnings and the return of the light.
2. **Quiet Reflection**: Winter is a time for quiet reflection and introspection. Set aside time each day for meditation, journaling, or simply sitting in silence. Use this time to connect with your inner self and gain clarity on your goals and desires.
3. **Nurturing Rituals**: Winter is a season for self-care and nurturing. Create rituals that nourish your body, mind, and spirit. This could include warm baths with essential oils, cozying up with a good book, or engaging in creative activities. Use this time to recharge and renew your energy.

Integrating Seasonal Rituals into Daily Life

To fully benefit from seasonal rituals, it's important to integrate them into your daily life. Here are some tips for making seasonal practices a regular part of your routine:

1. **Observe Nature**: Pay attention to the natural world around you and notice the changes in each season. Reflect on how these changes are mirrored in your own life and incorporate this awareness into your daily activities.
2. **Create Seasonal Altars**: Set up a small altar in your home that reflects the energy of each season. Use natural items, candles, and symbols that represent the season's themes. Change the altar with each new season to honor the cycle of the year.
3. **Seasonal Journaling**: Keep a journal to record your thoughts, reflections, and intentions for each season. Use it to track your progress, celebrate your achievements, and reflect on the lessons learned.

4. **Community Celebrations**: Join or create community celebrations for seasonal rituals. Gathering with others to honor the seasons can deepen your connection to the natural world and provide a sense of belonging and shared purpose.
5. **Mindful Eating**: Incorporate seasonal foods into your diet and be mindful of the natural cycles of growth and harvest. Eating seasonally helps you connect with the earth's rhythms and nourish your body with fresh, local produce.

Conclusion: Embracing the Cycles of Life

Seasonal rituals offer a powerful way to connect with the natural world and honor the cycles of life. By aligning your actions and intentions with the changing seasons, you can cultivate a deeper sense of harmony, balance, and well-being.

Embrace the practices that resonate with you and make them a regular part of your life. With each passing season, you will find that these rituals bring a sense of continuity, purpose, and connection to your spiritual journey.

May your journey through the seasons be filled with moments of reflection, celebration, and transformation. Let the cycles of nature guide you toward greater understanding, growth, and harmony, as you embrace the beauty and wisdom of each changing season.

Chapter 19: Balancing the Elements

The Fundamental Forces of Nature

The elements—Earth, Air, Fire, Water, and Spirit—are the fundamental forces that shape our world and influence our lives. Each element embodies unique qualities and energies that can be harnessed for personal growth, healing, and magickal work. Balancing these elements within ourselves and our environment is essential for achieving harmony and well-being. This chapter explores the art of balancing the elements, offering insights and practices to help you connect with these powerful forces and integrate them into your life.

Understanding the Elements

Before diving into the practices for balancing the elements, it's important to understand the characteristics and correspondences of each one. Each element has its own distinct energy and plays a crucial role in the natural world and our inner selves.

1. **Earth**: Earth is the element of stability, grounding, and physicality. It represents the material world, our bodies, and the structures that support us. Earth is associated with the physical realm, fertility, and abundance. It provides a foundation for growth and sustains life. Earth is nurturing, steadfast, and dependable.
2. **Air**: Air is the element of intellect, communication, and movement. It governs our thoughts, ideas, and the breath of life. Air is associated with clarity, creativity, and freedom. It inspires us to think, learn, and express ourselves. Air is light, adaptable, and ever-changing.
3. **Fire**: Fire is the element of energy, transformation, and passion. It represents the spark of life, creativity, and willpower. Fire is associated with action, courage, and purification. It drives us to pursue our goals and overcome challenges. Fire is dynamic, intense, and transformative.

4. **Water**: Water is the element of emotions, intuition, and healing. It governs our feelings, dreams, and the flow of life. Water is associated with empathy, compassion, and adaptability. It connects us to our inner selves and others. Water is fluid, nurturing, and soothing.
5. **Spirit**: Spirit, or Aether, is the element of unity, consciousness, and the divine. It represents the interconnectedness of all things and the essence of life. Spirit is associated with transcendence, enlightenment, and spiritual growth. It connects us to higher realms and our true nature. Spirit is ethereal, boundless, and eternal.

The Importance of Elemental Balance
Balancing the elements is crucial for achieving harmony within ourselves and our environment. When the elements are in balance, we experience physical health, emotional stability, mental clarity, and spiritual growth. However, imbalances can lead to various issues, such as feeling disconnected, overwhelmed, or stagnant.

For example, an excess of Earth energy may lead to rigidity and stubbornness, while a deficiency might cause instability and lack of focus. Too much Fire energy can result in anger and burnout, whereas too little may cause lethargy and lack of motivation. Balancing the elements helps us to navigate life with greater ease and resilience, allowing us to thrive in all aspects of our being.

Practices for Balancing the Elements
Here are some practical techniques to help you connect with and balance each element within yourself and your environment.

Balancing Earth

1. **Grounding Exercises**: Grounding connects you to the Earth's stabilizing energy. Spend time outdoors, walk barefoot on grass or soil, or sit quietly in nature. Visualize roots extending from your feet into the earth, anchoring you securely.
2. **Gardening**: Engage in gardening or tending to plants. This practice connects you with the cycles of nature and the nurturing energy of Earth. Planting, weeding, and harvesting help cultivate patience and appreciation for growth.

3. **Physical Activity**: Engage in physical activities that connect you to your body, such as yoga, hiking, or weightlifting. These activities help to strengthen your physical foundation and enhance your connection to the Earth.
4. **Nutrition**: Nourish your body with wholesome, grounding foods. Incorporate root vegetables, grains, and proteins into your diet. Eating mindfully and appreciating the food you consume fosters a deeper connection to the Earth element.

Balancing Air

1. **Breathwork**: Practice breathwork techniques to connect with the Air element. Deep breathing, alternate nostril breathing, and breath awareness exercises help to clear the mind and enhance mental clarity.
2. **Journaling**: Write down your thoughts, ideas, and reflections. Journaling helps to organize your thoughts and promotes self-expression. It also provides a space for creative exploration and problem-solving.

3. **Learning and Communication**: Engage in activities that stimulate your intellect and communication skills. Read books, take courses, or join discussions. Sharing ideas and learning from others helps to balance the Air element.
4. **Movement and Travel**: Embrace movement and change by exploring new places and experiences. Travel, even short trips, can refresh your perspective and invigorate your mind.

Balancing Fire

1. **Creative Expression**: Engage in creative activities that ignite your passion. Painting, dancing, writing, or any form of artistic expression helps to channel Fire energy constructively.
2. **Exercise and Movement**: Physical activities that raise your heart rate, such as running, martial arts, or aerobics, help to release excess Fire energy and maintain balance. These activities also boost confidence and motivation.

3. **Candle Gazing**: Practice candle gazing meditation. Light a candle and focus on the flame, visualizing it burning away negativity and igniting your inner light. This practice enhances concentration and purifies your energy.
4. **Setting Goals**: Set clear, achievable goals and take action toward them. Breaking down larger tasks into smaller steps helps maintain focus and drive. Celebrate your accomplishments to keep the Fire element balanced and energized.

Balancing Water

1. **Meditation and Visualization**: Practice meditation techniques that involve water imagery. Visualize yourself immersed in a calm, flowing river, allowing the water to wash away stress and emotional blockages.
2. **Hydration**: Ensure you drink plenty of water throughout the day. Staying hydrated supports your physical and emotional well-being. Infuse your water with herbs or fruits for added healing properties.

3. **Bath Rituals**: Take regular baths with salts, essential oils, or herbs. Soaking in water helps to relax and cleanse your body and mind. Use this time for reflection and emotional healing.
4. **Emotional Expression**: Allow yourself to fully experience and express your emotions. Journaling, talking to a trusted friend, or engaging in therapeutic activities like art or music can help process and release emotions.

Balancing Spirit

1. **Spiritual Practices**: Engage in regular spiritual practices that connect you with your higher self and the divine. This could include prayer, meditation, or rituals that resonate with your beliefs.
2. **Energy Healing**: Explore energy healing modalities such as Reiki, crystal healing, or chakra balancing. These practices help to align your energy and connect you with the Spirit element.

3. **Nature Connection**: Spend time in nature to connect with the Spirit element. Nature walks, stargazing, or simply sitting quietly outdoors can foster a sense of unity and transcendence.
4. **Mindfulness and Presence**: Practice mindfulness to stay present in the moment. Being fully aware of your thoughts, feelings, and surroundings helps to cultivate a deeper connection with Spirit.

Creating Elemental Balance in Your Environment

In addition to balancing the elements within yourself, it's important to create a balanced environment. Here are some tips for incorporating the elements into your living space:

1. **Earth**: Incorporate natural materials like wood, stone, and plants into your decor. Use earthy colors like green, brown, and beige. Ensure your space is organized and clutter-free to promote stability and grounding.

2. **Air**: Enhance airflow and ventilation in your home. Use light, airy fabrics and colors like white, blue, and pastel shades. Incorporate items that inspire creativity and intellectual stimulation, such as books and art.
3. **Fire**: Add elements of warmth and light to your space. Use candles, fireplaces, or lighting with warm tones. Incorporate colors like red, orange, and gold. Display items that evoke passion and energy, such as artwork or motivational quotes.
4. **Water**: Introduce water features like fountains or aquariums. Use calming colors like blue and turquoise. Incorporate reflective surfaces and soft, flowing fabrics. Create a serene atmosphere with items that evoke relaxation, such as soft lighting and soothing music.
5. **Spirit**: Create a sacred space for meditation and spiritual practice. Use items that have personal or spiritual significance, such as crystals, altars, or symbols. Ensure this space is quiet and free from distractions, allowing for deep connection and reflection.

Conclusion: Embracing Elemental Harmony

Balancing the elements is a journey of self-discovery and connection with the natural world. By integrating practices that honor and balance Earth, Air, Fire, Water, and Spirit, you can cultivate a harmonious and fulfilling life.

Embrace the practices that resonate with you and make them a regular part of your daily routine. With dedication and mindfulness, you will find that balancing the elements enhances your well-being, enriches your spiritual journey, and fosters a deeper connection with the world around you.

May your journey in balancing the elements be filled with moments of insight, transformation, and profound peace. Let the wisdom of the elements guide you toward greater harmony and understanding, where you can fully embrace your true potential and the beauty of each element's gifts.

Chapter 20: Living a Life of Natural Magick

Embracing the Everyday Enchantment

Natural magick is not just a series of rituals or spells; it is a way of life. It is an art of weaving the sacred into the mundane, transforming everyday experiences into opportunities for connection, growth, and wonder. Living a life of natural magick means seeing the world through enchanted eyes, recognizing the divine in all things, and harnessing the energies of nature to enhance your life and the lives of others. This chapter explores the principles and practices for integrating natural magick into every aspect of your existence, helping you to create a life that is both magickal and profoundly fulfilling.

The Principles of Natural Magick

At the heart of natural magick are a few guiding principles that help you align with the forces of nature and the universe. Understanding and embracing these principles is essential for living a life of natural magick:

1. **Interconnectedness**: Recognize that all things are connected. The web of life binds us to the earth, the elements, and each other. Our actions ripple outwards, affecting the whole. This understanding fosters a sense of responsibility and compassion for all living beings.
2. **Cyclical Nature**: Honor the cycles of nature—day and night, the seasons, the phases of the moon. These cycles mirror our own lives, filled with periods of growth, rest, and renewal. Aligning with these rhythms brings balance and harmony.
3. **Intentional Living**: Live with intention and mindfulness. Every action, thought, and word carries energy and power. By setting clear intentions, you can direct this energy towards positive outcomes and manifest your desires.
4. **Harmony and Balance**: Strive for balance in all things—within yourself, your relationships, and your environment. Balance the elements, your physical and spiritual needs, and your work and rest. This harmony leads to a peaceful and empowered life.

5. **Reverence for Nature**: Hold a deep respect and reverence for the natural world. Nature is a source of wisdom, healing, and inspiration. By honoring and protecting the earth, you nurture your connection to its magick.

Daily Practices for Living Natural Magick

Integrating natural magick into your daily life can be both simple and transformative. Here are some practices to help you live a life infused with magick:

1. **Morning Rituals**: Begin your day with a morning ritual that sets a positive tone and intention. This could include meditation, journaling, or a simple prayer. Light a candle and express gratitude for the new day, inviting positive energies to guide you.
2. **Mindful Presence**: Practice mindfulness throughout your day. Be fully present in each moment, whether you're eating, walking, or working. Notice the details of your surroundings, the sensations in your body, and the flow of your breath. Mindfulness connects you to the magick of the present moment.

3. **Nature Connection**: Spend time in nature daily, even if it's just a short walk in the park or sitting in your garden. Observe the changing seasons, the patterns of the clouds, and the songs of the birds. Nature has a way of grounding us and reminding us of the beauty and magick of life.
4. **Herbal Allies**: Incorporate herbs into your daily routine for their magickal and healing properties. Drink herbal teas, cook with fresh herbs, and use essential oils for aromatherapy. Each herb carries unique energies that can enhance your well-being and spiritual practice.
5. **Sacred Spaces**: Create sacred spaces in your home where you can retreat, reflect, and connect with your inner self. An altar with items that hold personal significance, such as crystals, candles, and symbols, can serve as a focal point for your magickal work and daily rituals.

6. **Intentional Meals**: Treat your meals as a sacred practice. Prepare and eat your food with mindfulness and gratitude. Bless your food, recognizing it as a gift from the earth that nourishes your body and spirit.
7. **Affirmations and Mantras**: Use affirmations and mantras to focus your mind and align with your intentions. Repeat them throughout the day to reinforce positive thoughts and energies. For example, "I am grounded and connected to the earth," or "I attract love and abundance."
8. **Moon Phases**: Align your activities with the phases of the moon. The new moon is a time for setting intentions and new beginnings, the waxing moon for growth and action, the full moon for celebration and manifestation, and the waning moon for release and reflection.
9. **Gratitude Practice**: Cultivate an attitude of gratitude. Each evening, reflect on the things you are grateful for. This practice shifts your focus to the positive aspects of your life and attracts more of what you appreciate.

Seasonal Celebrations

Honoring the cycles of nature through seasonal celebrations is a cornerstone of natural magick. These celebrations mark the turning points of the year and offer opportunities to connect deeply with the energies of each season:

1. **Spring Equinox (Ostara)**: Celebrate renewal and rebirth. Decorate your home with flowers, plant seeds, and set new intentions. Reflect on the areas of your life where you want to experience growth and renewal.
2. **Summer Solstice (Litha)**: Celebrate the peak of light and abundance. Light a bonfire or candles to honor the sun. Reflect on your achievements and express gratitude for the abundance in your life. Share a feast with loved ones and spend time outdoors.
3. **Autumn Equinox (Mabon)**: Celebrate balance and harvest. Reflect on the past year, acknowledging your successes and lessons learned. Perform a gratitude ritual and share a meal made from seasonal produce. Release what no longer serves you.

4. **Winter Solstice (Yule)**: Celebrate the return of the light. Decorate with evergreen branches and candles. Reflect on your hopes and intentions for the new year. Engage in quiet reflection and self-care, honoring the need for rest and renewal.

Magick in the Mundane

Living a life of natural magick means finding magick in the mundane. Here are some ways to bring magick into everyday activities:

1. **Cleaning as Cleansing**: View cleaning your home as a magickal practice. Use natural cleaning products infused with essential oils and herbs. As you clean, visualize negative energy being swept away and your space being filled with positive, vibrant energy.
2. **Bathing as Ritual**: Turn your daily bath or shower into a ritual. Add sea salt, herbs, or essential oils to the water. As you cleanse your body, imagine washing away stress and negativity, leaving you refreshed and purified.

3. **Commuting as Meditation**: Use your commute as a time for meditation or reflection. Listen to calming music, practice deep breathing, or silently repeat affirmations. Transform this routine task into a moment of peace and mindfulness.
4. **Gardening as Magick**: Approach gardening as a magickal practice. Bless your seeds and plants, infuse them with intentions, and communicate with the spirits of the plants and the earth. Gardening becomes a way to connect with nature and manifest your desires.
5. **Crafting as Spellwork**: View crafting and creative projects as opportunities for spellwork. Infuse your creations with magickal intent, whether you're knitting, painting, or cooking. Each act of creation becomes a manifestation of your intentions.

Building a Magickal Community

Community is an important aspect of living a life of natural magick. Connecting with like-minded individuals can provide support, inspiration, and a sense of belonging. Here are some ways to build a magickal community:

1. **Join Groups**: Seek out local or online groups focused on natural magick, spirituality, or witchcraft. Participate in gatherings, workshops, and discussions to share knowledge and experiences.
2. **Create Rituals Together**: Organize seasonal celebrations, full moon rituals, or meditation circles with friends or community members. Performing rituals together can deepen your connection and amplify the magick.
3. **Share Knowledge**: Share your knowledge and experiences with others. Teach a workshop, write a blog, or lead a discussion group. Contributing to the community helps to strengthen it and spread the wisdom of natural magick.
4. **Support Each Other**: Offer support and encouragement to fellow practitioners. Celebrate each other's successes, provide a listening ear during challenges, and collaborate on magickal projects. A supportive community enhances everyone's magickal practice.

Conclusion: Embracing the Magickal Life

Living a life of natural magick is a journey of continuous growth, discovery, and connection. By embracing the principles of natural magick and integrating magickal practices into your daily life, you can create a life that is rich with meaning, wonder, and harmony.

Remember that magick is not confined to rituals and spells; it is present in every moment, waiting to be recognized and harnessed. Approach each day with curiosity and reverence, and you will find that the world is full of magickal possibilities.

May your journey in living a life of natural magick be filled with joy, inspiration, and profound transformation. Let the wisdom of nature and the power of your intentions guide you toward a life that is truly enchanted and fulfilling. Embrace the magick within and around you, and let it illuminate your path.

Recommended Materials

Books and References

1. **"The Complete Book of Incense, Oils and Brews" by Scott Cunningham** - A comprehensive guide on creating and using magickal potions, oils, and incense.
2. **"The Green Witch: Your Complete Guide to the Natural Magic of Herbs, Flowers, Essential Oils, and More" by Arin Murphy-Hiscock** - A practical resource for incorporating green witchcraft into daily life.
3. **"The Spiral Dance: A Rebirth of the Ancient Religion of the Great Goddess" by Starhawk** - An essential read on the principles and practices of modern witchcraft.
4. **"Sacred Earth Celebrations: A Guide to Rituals and Practices" by Glennie Kindred** - A guide to creating rituals that honor the Earth's cycles.
5. **"The Book of Crystal Spells: Magical Uses for Stones, Crystals, Minerals...and Even Sand" by Ember Grant** - A useful reference for incorporating crystals into your magickal practice.

Tools and Supplies

1. **Candles** - Various colors for different magickal purposes. White for purification, green for growth, red for passion, etc.
2. **Crystals** - Clear quartz, amethyst, rose quartz, black tourmaline, and others for healing, protection, and enhancing energy.
3. **Herbs** - Sage, lavender, rosemary, chamomile, and others for rituals, teas, and cleansing.
4. **Essential Oils** - Lavender, peppermint, eucalyptus, frankincense, and other oils for aromatherapy and anointing.
5. **Incense and Burners** - Sage, sandalwood, frankincense, and other incense for cleansing and creating sacred spaces.

Journaling and Reflection

1. **Dream Journal** - A dedicated journal for recording and interpreting dreams.
2. **Gratitude Journal** - A journal for daily reflections on gratitude and positive affirmations.
3. **Ritual Diary** - A diary for documenting rituals, spells, and personal experiences.

Altar Supplies

1. **Altar Cloths** - Different colors and fabrics for various seasons and rituals.
2. **Statues or Symbols** - Representations of deities, spirit guides, or personal symbols of power.
3. **Offerings** - Items like flowers, fruits, coins, or other meaningful objects to place on your altar.
4. **Candle Holders** - For safely burning candles during rituals and meditations.
5. **Chalice or Bowl** - For holding water, offerings, or other ritual substances.

Practical Tools

1. **Mortar and Pestle** - For grinding herbs and other ingredients.
2. **Cauldron** - A small cauldron for burning herbs or mixing potions.
3. **Athame or Ritual Knife** - A ceremonial knife used in rituals for directing energy.
4. **Tarot or Oracle Cards** - For divination and gaining insights.
5. **Pendulum** - For dowsing and communication with the subconscious mind.

Outdoor and Gardening Supplies

1. **Gardening Tools** - Trowel, gloves, and other tools for planting and tending to herbs and flowers.
2. **Planters and Pots** - For growing herbs and plants indoors or on balconies.
3. **Compost Bin** - For recycling organic waste and creating nutrient-rich soil.
4. **Bird Feeder** - To attract and feed birds, fostering a connection with nature.

Clothing and Accessories

1. **Ritual Robes** - Comfortable and meaningful clothing for performing rituals.
2. **Jewelry** - Amulets, talismans, or other jewelry imbued with personal significance.
3. **Herb Pouches** - Small bags for carrying herbs and crystals for protection or energy.

Digital Resources

1. **Meditation Apps** - Apps like Headspace or Insight Timer for guided meditations.
2. **Moon Phase Tracker** - Apps or websites that track the moon phases and astrological events.

3. **Online Courses and Workshops** - Platforms offering courses on natural magick, herbalism, and spiritual practices.

Additional Supplies

1. **Natural Cleaning Products** - Eco-friendly cleaning products for purifying your space.
2. **Baskets and Containers** - For collecting herbs, flowers, and natural items.
3. **Muslin Bags** - For making herbal sachets or tea blends.
4. **Water Filter** - For ensuring clean, pure water in rituals and daily use.
5. **Wind Chimes** - To enhance the energy flow and create a peaceful ambiance.

By gathering these recommended materials, you can create a well-equipped and inspiring environment to support your journey in living a life of natural magick. Each item serves to deepen your connection to the natural world and enrich your magickal practice, helping you to embrace the sacred in every moment.

A Letter to My Dear Reader

Dear Reader,

I want to extend my heartfelt gratitude to you for choosing to read "Natural Magick: Embracing the Sacred in Everyday Life." Your support means the world to me, and I am truly honored that you have welcomed this book into your life.

Writing this book has been a labor of love, inspired by my deep connection to the natural world and my desire to share the beauty and power of natural magick with others. It is my hope that the insights, rituals, and practices within these pages have resonated with you, offering inspiration and guidance on your own magickal journey.

As you continue to explore the wonders of natural magick, I would be immensely grateful if you could take a moment to share your thoughts about this book on Amazon. Your review not only helps other readers discover "Natural Magick," but it also provides valuable feedback that can guide future works.

Writing a review is simple and only takes a few moments, but its impact is profound. Honest reviews help other potential readers make informed decisions and ensure that those who are seeking a deeper connection with natural magick can find the resources they need.

Here are a few points you might consider when writing your review:

- What aspects of the book did you find most inspiring or useful?
- How has "Natural Magick" influenced your personal practice or perspective?
- Are there any particular chapters or rituals that stood out to you?
- Would you recommend this book to others who are interested in natural magick and why?

Your words have the power to inspire and guide others on their own paths, just as this book has hopefully inspired you. Your support through a review would mean so much to me and to the wider community of readers.

Thank you once again for being a part of this journey. I am deeply appreciative of your support and wish you all the best as you continue to embrace the sacred in everyday life.

With warmest regards,

Dorian Bloodmoon

About the Author

Dorian Bloodmoon, a gifted occultist in his late twenties, has swiftly gained recognition for his profound understanding and innovative practices in demonology and ceremonial magic. Despite his youth, Dorian has immersed himself in the study of the Lesser Key of Solomon and the spirits of the Ars Goetia, blending meticulous historical research with modern-day applications. His writings make intricate magical rituals accessible and ethically sound, earning him a dedicated following among both novice and seasoned practitioners. With a reputation for his rigorous scholarship and practical insights, Dorian continues to inspire and guide a new generation of occult enthusiasts around the world.

Made in the USA
Columbia, SC
31 January 2025

53035721R10120